An Unconditional Relationship To Life

The Odyssey Of A Young American Spiritual Teacher

Andrew Cohen

MOKSHA PRESS 1995

OTHER BOOKS BY ANDREW COHEN

Enlightenment Is a Secret

Autobiography of an Awakening

My Master Is My Self

CONTENTS

THE DISCOVERY OF A BIGGER VIEW

THE VISCERAL RESPONSE

THE SCIENCE OF ENLIGHTENMENT

THE UNKNOWN CAN ONLY BE UNKNOWN

I want to thank Kathy Bayer from the bottom of my heart for all the love and care she put into the creation of this book that occurred in the midst of the unbroken chaos that has become my life.

PREFACE

*I*n the time that we are living in, there is an almost profound disinterest in most to come to a final reckoning of the human predicament when faced with the possibility of unconditional transformation. An air of cynicism pervades the hearts and minds of many. It is because so few believe that it's actually possible to go all the way that an endless array of curious rationalizations for not needing to do so have become so prevalent in our time.

The word "truth" has always been dangerous territory and continues to be in the modern world, even in spite of the seeming open-mindedness of the so-called new age. The endless need of the individual to be an independent expression of that which is singular creates an environment that makes radical transcendence beyond any personal significance extremely difficult.

I have continuously stated that Truth is not an object, thought or feeling of any kind, but in fact is only that perspective of reality that is so unobstructed that it reveals the true and right relationship of all things. It is in the pursuit and discovery of that perspective alone that salvation lies for the individual and ultimately for the race as a whole. There is no other way. There is no other way only because as long as the needs of the personal are allowed to subordinate the necessity of the realization of the Truth itself, true salvation is an impossibility.

INTRODUCTION

The pain of the consequences of my inability to compromise in simple yet profound matters of the heart has been and continues to be great. What do I mean by matters of the heart? I mean to propose that if Love that frees the human spirit is not founded upon true integrity and consistency in that integrity in a human soul, then its result cannot truly liberate.

Truth is the revelation and intuitive recognition of the way itself. Love is the emotional experience of profound surrender that is the ecstasy of transcendence. The discovery of Truth without Love is empty and the experience of Love without Truth is always superficial.

A strange predicament—often condemned for my unwillingness to compromise in these matters of the heart—compels me to share my life with those who are interested in trying to understand the relationship between Love and Truth.

WHAT IS IT ALL ABOUT?

Chapter 1

WHAT IS IT ALL ABOUT?

Kathmandu, Nepal   February 1991

"But you couldn't be enlightened!" the Rinpoche said emphatically.

"Why not?" I asked.

"Because you can't read my mind, fly through the air or appear in ten places at the same time."

"But Rinpoche, that has nothing to do with enlightenment!" I exclaimed.

The Rinpoche, a stocky man in his early forties, got up out of his chair and sat in the chair next to mine. Putting my hands in his own, he pulled me very close to him so that our noses were almost touching. With his bright, shining eyes staring directly into mine, he seemed to try to overwhelm me with his intensity.

"Also Andrew," he said, "you mustn't go around saying you're enlightened."

Not moving, looking directly into his eyes, I said, "Rinpoche, I never said I was enlightened."

"I know," he insisted. "You mustn't go around saying you're enlightened. It's not right."

Repeating myself, I said, "Rinpoche, I never said I was enlightened."

Repeating himself yet again, he said a third time, "You mustn't go around saying you're enlightened."

Again I responded, "Rinpoche, I do not go around saying I'm enlightened. But if people ask me questions, I can't deny my own experience."

As I left the Rinpoche's house and walked out into the bright morning light of the Kathmandu Valley, I was struck by the beauty of the snowcapped peaks of the Himalayan mountain range in the distance. On the taxi ride back to Thamel on the other side of Kathmandu, I recalled that one of my female students who had formerly been a disciple of the late Chogyam Trungpa Rinpoche had been asked by him one night to go to bed with the Rinpoche I had just been speaking with. In fact, she had been third in line for him on a night of drunken escapades.

We drove back to our hotel through the mud, dust and stench of the dirty Kathmandu streets. As the taxi bumped along, I scratched my head and wondered, as I had so many times over the years since I'd begun teaching, "What is it all about?"

I had recently finished three weeks of teaching in

Bodhgaya in northern India, the site of the Buddha's awakening, and was now spending two weeks in Kathmandu meeting Tibetan lamas and rinpoches. I went to Kathmandu that year because while in Bodhgaya, an English woman who had come to my teachings several times had told me that my teachings were very similar to the Dzogchen teachings of Tibetan Buddhism. She then arranged for me to meet one of the greatest living exponents of Dzogchen, Chatrul Rinpoche. The Rinpoche was an extraordinary and beautiful looking man in his late seventies who had spent over thirty years in retreat. I was inspired by our meeting and he encouraged me to come to Kathmandu to see him again.

At that point in my life, my ongoing investigation into the nature and expression of enlightenment had created a very tenuous situation in my relationship with my own guru, the now well-known H.W.L. Poonja. Over a five-year period, I had become gradually more and more confused by the discrepancies in his conduct with me and others, and the concerns this raised compelled me to try to find answers to some very difficult questions. Questions such as: What is the relationship between Love and Truth? What is the relationship between spiritual awakening and human conduct? At that time, even though I was reeling from the endless inconsistencies and ensuing confusion that seemed to be the expression of enlightenment in my own guru and in so many modern masters, I had not yet fully come to terms with the fact that my own pursuit of sanity and unwillingness to compromise my integrity would soon lead to the dissolution of my relationship with my own teacher and would propel me into the unknown like never before.

Chapter 2

ODD ENCOUNTERS

That February in Kathmandu was fascinating and seemed to pose more questions than it answered. News of the fact that I had had a good meeting with Chatrul Rinpoche in Bodhgaya and again in Kathmandu had circulated in the local Buddhist community and had caused a small but not insignificant stir. Many, it seemed, were unwilling to believe or accept the fact that I, a relatively young westerner (I was thirty-five at the time and also not a Buddhist), had been recognized as a teacher in my own right by a highly respected Tibetan master.

At the end of our first meeting in Bodhgaya, after fiercely questioning me to ascertain the validity of my attainment, the Rinpoche proclaimed, "Please bring countless beings to this path." The translator for that initial meeting was a middle-aged western woman whom I had been told was a practitioner of Tibetan Buddhism for many years. She had come to one of my teachings in Bodhgaya and had walked out halfway through, apparently outraged at some of the things I had been saying. Not surprisingly, therefore, she appeared to be angry while translating for the dialogue between the Rinpoche and myself, and interestingly enough, omitted the Rinpoche's last statement. After leaving that first meeting, a French woman who had been there told me what the translator had neglected to tell me, and the following afternoon a western monk who had also been present during that meeting told one of my students to please communicate the Rinpoche's last words to me. This kind of antagonism from many in the spiritual world has been my constant companion since I began teaching in Rishikesh in northern India in 1986.

One day while I was resting in my hotel room in Thamel, out of the blue the phone rang. A westerner who had been living in Kathmandu for years and was a fixture in the local Buddhist community said she had a message for me from Dzongsar Rinpoche, an internationally respected, young, up-and-coming Tibetan lama who is a tulku (a reincarnation of an enlightened lama). Apparently the Lama was offering me a challenge, and through the caller was proposing five questions that he wanted me to answer. This is interesting, I thought. The five questions were:

1. What is ultimate view?
2. Is your enlightenment produced?
3. *Is* your enlightenment wisdom or does it *have* wisdom?

4. What kind of action should a practitioner adopt as a practitioner?

5. What is the character of wisdom?

After I put the phone down, I turned to one of my students and said, "Please write down the following answers:

1. No question of problem, no question of no problem.
2. I don't know what he means by 'produced'.
3. It *is* wisdom.
4. Right action.
5. Love."

The following day, I asked two of my students to go see the young Lama to arrange an appointment so that I could meet his challenge face to face. They went to the main monastery of the late, great Dilgo Khyentse Rinpoche, one of the largest monasteries in Kathmandu. It was filled with activity because it was the middle of the Tibetan New Year and many pujas (rituals and ceremonies) were in progress. My students called for an appointment and arrived at the agreed upon time. After a long wait, the young Rinpoche suddenly appeared and ran down the stairs toward the bathroom, followed by his western student who informed them that he would meet with them shortly. Upon his return, they followed him into his room, which was fully adorned with Tibetan paintings, butterlamps, Buddhist statues and a throne. Twenty-five of his students, most of whom were western, were in the room.

After ignoring my students for some time, while looking out the window in the opposite direction, he asked them what they wanted. They told him that they were my students, that they had come on my request to respond to his challenge and to arrange a convenient time for us to meet and speak about the questions that he had posed. He said that he didn't have any time. My students told him they were sure that I would be happy to accommodate him and would be willing to meet him any time and any place, and reminded him that it had been he who had initiated the challenge. Then the Rinpoche suddenly leapt up on his throne and shouted, "I don't even have time to piss!" The meeting never happened.

We hired a translator for my second meeting with Chatrul Rinpoche, which took place at his monastery outside Kathmandu. During the bus ride on the way there, the translator, an English woman in her late forties, sat next to me. She was a Buddhist nun and had been deeply involved in Tibetan practice and study for many years. I remember being surprised when, in the midst of a lively and pleasant conversation about "crazy wisdom" and the abuses of power of some spiritual teachers, she suddenly exclaimed, "Everything that the lamas do is for our benefit. They are so compassionate." She went on to explain to me that all the lamas of high attainment could walk through walls whenever they wished, including Chatrul Rinpoche himself!

Chapter 3

THE QUALITY OF ATTENTION

I had for some time been perplexed about how and why tales of miraculous and superhuman occurrences were intermingled with the unfolding of profound revelation and rare insight in the traditional religions of the world. In Tibetan Buddhism, for example, I was amazed how obviously absurd mythical stories of the ancient Tibetan adepts could exist side by side with some of the most exquisitely refined and profoundly subtle teachings ever given. That January in Bodhgaya, I found one way to understand.

Genuine spiritual awakening is a shift in perception from the gross to the subtle. From a gross and unrefined state of perception, the individual draws conclusions about that which is being perceived. As the individual's perception, through spiritual awakening, becomes more subtle and more refined, their conclusions about that which is being perceived also become more subtle and more distinct. This reveals greater depth, width and breadth of that which is being perceived than was previously observed.

This movement from the gross to the subtle continues from subtle to even more subtle and refined, and continues to deepen until ideally the individual becomes firmly established in a condition of subtlety of perception and cognition that is stable and irrevocable.

The awesome depth and subtlety discovered in profound spiritual revelation is, due to the generally gross condition of perception, out of reach for most. Not only is it usually out of reach, but the magnitude of that subtlety and depth is almost impossible to recognize unless one is able to achieve some degree of direct insight oneself. Even then, the individual's ability to discriminate is entirely determined by how far they have actually gone. Therefore, it's plausible that stories of miraculous and superhuman feats could, by their dramatic and concept-challenging nature, indicate to any human being the inconceivable subtlety and vast depth of perception attained through extraordinary spiritual transformation.

As a result of the ongoing events in my own life and speeded up by my meetings with different teachers from different traditions, something even more significant dawned on me. It became apparent in ever new ways that it was the *interpretation* of our experience rather than the fact of experience itself that determined real depth and true wisdom. It was the ability to interpret, decipher and ultimately be able to make extremely subtle distinctions in the whole realm of human experience, thought and feeling that determined the ultimate depth of insight or wisdom that resulted from the fact of experience itself. Mere experience in and of itself did not, I was coming to discover over and over again, necessarily result in the attainment of any lasting insight or depth of understanding.

The importance of this became more clear as I began to see that *the conclusions we draw about that which is true are entirely based on our ability to perceive the depth, width and breadth of subtlety in that which is being perceived.* This means that the quality of attention that has been either cultivated or realized by the perceiver ultimately determines the degree of subtlety of understanding that the individual is capable of.

Chapter 4

THOUGHT DOES NOT CREATE KARMA

I had one other important meeting that February that was interesting. A private meeting was arranged at extremely short notice with Urgyen Tulku, who is considered by Tibetans to be a living Buddha. It had been suggested to me by another western practitioner of Tibetan Buddhism that I meet him as he is deemed to be, like Chatrul Rinpoche, one of the few fully awakened living adepts of Dzogchen. The meeting was difficult. Initially the Lama asked me several questions that created confusion as I was unfamiliar with much of the terminology that he was using. For example, I found out later that in Tibetan Buddhism, simply put, the word "mind" refers to awareness itself; whereas in my own teaching, "mind" refers to the movement of thought alone. This made direct communication slow and difficult. At one point he asked me if there was still identification with the story or events that unfolded in the midst of dreaming. I said yes, but went on to explain how that was not necessarily an indication of freedom or bondage.

I had come to the realization that the movement of thought, and any kind of internal response to that movement, in and of itself in no way necessarily indicated the depth or level of spiritual attainment. In fact, I had discovered something very interesting. It was only the individual's ability to respond spontaneously and fearlessly to life *in spite of* the experience of thought and feeling that ultimately demonstrated true freedom and real detachment. I tried to explain this in greater detail, but time and circumstance didn't allow the opportunity to communicate it clearly enough. Then the meeting became even more confusing. The Lama said that as long as there was the arising of thought, then full awakening had not been achieved. "Is there still the arising of thought?" he asked me. Looking out the window and motioning toward the clouds moving over the valley in the distance, I said, "If there are clouds in the sky, then there is the arising of thought."

At the end of the meeting, the Lama said to me, "Very good. Continue and eventually you'll be able to fly through the air and read people's minds." I thanked him for seeing me, but I couldn't help feeling perplexed by our interchange and slightly dissatisfied as there was not more time to clarify these matters with greater depth. I was surprised to hear a lama of his stature equating a fully awakened condition with a silent mind. For a long time, I had been convinced that there was not necessarily any direct relationship between the experience of the nonarising of thought and the event of profound awakening. When I pursued this question later with Chatrul Rinpoche, he agreed:

> Buddha mind is not like a rock that has no kind of thoughts, nothing arising. But through the ultimate realization, the Buddha realization, then they realize that these thoughts have no essence. They may arise, but they understand them. They have perfect realization of them, but they have no clinging to them. Other than a rock, everything has some kind of ideation arising. But with the Buddha we call it wisdom. It is called wisdom. It is not called thought because there is no clinging. He has thoroughly understood them, he has thoroughly realized them, so that is what is called Buddha. Just to have no thoughts is not very special.

That January in Bodhgaya, quite a stir was created amongst some of the western Buddhist practitioners when word got out that I had said during one of my teachings that thought doesn't create karma. What I meant by this, and what I explained in detail at the time, is that the mere arising of thought in and of itself *need not* create karma. This point is of profound importance to anybody who is seriously interested in emancipation from fear, delusion and ignorance.

The mere presence of thought in and of itself means nothing. That means thought and the movement of thought do not necessarily indicate anything about the thinker. Like photographs in a photo album, thoughts are only abstract representations of reality—historical references and prior conclusions based on past experience. They have no independent self-existence. That means that there is no significance in their mere presence except that which we choose to give them through our own volition, conscious or unconscious. *We are what we do and not what we think.* That is the whole point. Liberation can be realized in the discovery of this alone. On an intellectual level this is not too difficult to understand, but practically speaking this kind of teaching often takes many years for the practitioner to fully realize for themselves.

Final acceptance of the fact that *thought is not self* represents the potential of final liberation from fear, delusion and ignorance. If thought in fact did have independent self-existence, and its mere arising automatically meant something about the individual, then that would mean there was really no way out of the endless misery and distortion of actuality that belief in the independent self-existence of thought creates. The importance of this point cannot be overstated. So many spiritual practitioners of different faiths live in fear of the arising of thought, because out of ignorance they are endlessly drawing conclusions about the nature of their own identity based on the mere arising of specific thoughts.

To live in fear of the arising of thought is the intentional practice of superstition. If we are convinced of the self-existing reality of thought, then we will constantly live in fear of specific thoughts and endlessly suffer in our desire for the presence of others. Our actions will express this common form of spiritual slavery and will demonstrate fear, delusion and ignorance. Final emancipation from the illusion of the independent self-existence of thought reveals to the individual that they have always had the freedom to choose, but due to ignorance haven't realized it.

IMPERSONAL ENLIGHTENMENT

Chapter 5

Impersonal Enlightenment

By that February in Kathmandu, I had been teaching for five years and had met thousands of seekers after Truth. Over those years, I discovered something that shocked me. I became aware of the fact that most individuals who were actively seeking for spiritual liberation tended to do so in a way that was profoundly self-centered. For most seekers, spiritual longing and experience was fundamentally a personal matter. It appeared, in fact, that in the end many spiritual seekers were not all that different from those who were not on a spiritual path, in the sense that they seemed for the most part to be as self-centered as everyone else. This self-preoccupation in spiritual seekers usually took the form of a very narrow-minded and self-centered relationship with enlightenment. In general, it seemed that the path of spiritual liberation was pursued in a way that emphasized the emancipation of the individual rather than the human race as a whole.

Over time, I had come to see that the desire for enlightenment was far more than a personal matter. I began to recognize that that desire was the expression of an impersonal, evolutionary impulse in the race as a whole that manifested itself in the individual as a yearning for transcendence, a longing for the experience of deep and profound wholeness. Some individuals experienced the movement of this evolutionary impulse with great intensity, others experienced this impulse in a milder form and in some it was not experienced at all. Too many who became aware of the movement of this impulse in themselves tended to overpersonalize its significance, and in so doing often obscured the *impersonal nature* of its essence. Because of this, the larger implications of the discovery of that impulse, which always pointed to the evolution of the race as a whole, often remained unrecognized.

This had a profound impact on me as a teacher and ultimately completely transformed my message. Indeed, that the individual's desire for awakening could never exist in isolation became the very foundation of my teaching. It was at this point that I began to call all approaches to enlightenment that stressed the awakening of the individual alone *Personal Enlightenment* and all approaches in which the awakening of the individual could never be separated from the awakening of the race as a whole *Impersonal Enlightenment.*

Chapter 6

A STATE OF CONSTANT REVOLUTION

Curious to meet me, a western couple who had lived in Kathmandu for many years and who were practicing Buddhists invited me to their house to teach informally for two evenings. My reviews were mixed, but they both liked me and invited some of my students and me over for dinner a week later. That evening turned out to be a fascinating one indeed, and helped to bring me to a deeper understanding of the ongoing evolution of my own teaching. I had recently come to new conclusions about the significance of form and structure and the role that they played in the spiritual life.

For a long time I had been wary of the form and structure of organized religion. It appeared to be suffocating, life inhibiting and almost always seemed to stifle the unconditional and absolute expression of the Truth itself. But after teaching for three years, it became obvious that when a significant number of human beings come together to express the force of evolution, form and structure become an inevitable necessity. I came to this conclusion only after much reservation. Then I discovered something I hadn't considered before: if religious structure is *constantly* being informed by the light of the living realization of those involved, then that structure itself would become the very expression of *evolution in action*. If this was so, then that structure would not stifle the unconditional and absolute expression of the Truth itself, but would be the very manifestation of it.

The couple who had invited me to dinner had also invited an American man in his late thirties who had been a Buddhist practitioner for many years. As the evening unfolded, I described the conclusions I had come to about approaching enlightenment from an impersonal versus a personal perspective. We then discussed the similarity of my ideas with the two main schools of Buddhism, the Hinayana and the Mahayana. Simply put, it is said that the Hinayana path is the lesser vehicle because it emphasizes individual enlightenment and that the Mahayana path is the greater vehicle because it emphasizes the enlightenment of all sentient beings. It was fascinating for me to find that I had, through my own teaching experience, gradually come to seemingly similar conclusions as those stressed in the Mahayana teachings. This is what interested me so much about Tibetan Buddhism.

Then my hosts' American friend made a bold and provocative claim. While describing to me his impressions of the actual manifestation of the Mahayana teachings in

Tibetan Buddhism, he stated that they were not living up to the Mahayana ideal of giving the enlightenment of the whole greater importance than the enlightenment of the individual. We both agreed that for enlightened religious structure to have a truly all-embracing impact on those involved, it was imperative that it affect the entire range of human relationship.

According to my hosts' friend, what was being practiced within the huge medieval structure of Tibetan Buddhism was the pursuit of personal enlightenment, while the very structures, it seemed, within which that pursuit was occurring remained largely unquestioned. This became clear as he described in detail how the family lives of many great, undoubtedly enlightened lamas and rinpoches were cauldrons of the very same kind of intrigue and confusion that occurred in the secular world. For example, he told me a tale about Chatrul Rinpoche's beautiful daughter that seemed to be a cosmic Tibetan version of a modern soap opera.

One of Chatrul Rinpoche's teachers, the great master of Dzogchen Dudjom Rinpoche, had died. The first son of his second marriage, who had taken his father's place, swept Chatrul Rinpoche's daughter, who at the time was a nun, off her feet. He stole her away, the story goes, to his mother's house in Kathmandu at the same time that ceremonies honoring his father were taking place. Shortly thereafter, she became pregnant. She had loved his father, Dudjom

Rinpoche, and apparently was under the impression that she would be giving birth to his reincarnation. After a few months, Dudjom Rinpoche's son left to teach in France. While there, he claimed that he had a letter from his deceased father describing whom he should marry, saying it was a Ladakhi princess. The princess joined him in France where they married. Chatrul Rinpoche's daughter only heard through someone else that her man had left her. Dudjom Rinpoche's second wife then found a child in Kathmandu whom she claimed was the true reincarnation of her deceased husband. Chatrul Rinpoche refused to recognize the child. In spite of that, Dudjom Rinpoche's wife got permission from the Dalai Lama to recognize the child in Kathmandu as the true reincarnation of Dudjom Rinpoche.

This fascinated me. If this was true, it meant that while the Mahayana emphasis on the liberation of all sentient beings before oneself was commonly expounded, the radical, impersonal implications inherent in that teaching were either not recognized, or if recognized, were possibly not truly being pursued. If they were, then the full weight of the enlightened vision would be made to fall on every aspect of human life.

Indeed, it seemed that for religious structures not to become fixed in any way that would allow stagnation or that could inhibit the unfettered and unbroken evolution of the race as a whole, they would have to remain in a state of constant revolution.

A CRISIS
OF TRUST

Chapter 7

Fullness or Emptiness?

"When I was sixteen years old, the most extraordinary thing happened to me. Late one night as I was talking with my mother, for no apparent reason I began to experience a completely new and unimaginable condition. My consciousness began to expand in all directions simultaneously and I experienced what could only be called revelation. Tears profusely poured out of my eyes and my throat repeatedly opened and closed for no reason. I was feeling completely overwhelmed and intoxicated by Love and was struck by a sense of awe and wonder that is impossible to describe. I suddenly knew without any doubt that there was no such thing as death and that life itself had no beginning and no end. I saw that all of life was intimately connected and inseparable. It became clear that there was no such thing as individuality separate from that one Self that was all of life. The glory and majesty in the cosmic unity that was revealing itself to me was completely overwhelming. I could hardly speak. My mother told me years later that I had said to her at the time not to worry, that I was not unhappy, and that this used to happen to me often when I was a child. In the midst of this explosion I was struck by what seemed to be a message that came directly from the revelation itself. That message was: if you give your life to me *alone* you have nothing to fear. Disoriented, it took me several days to recover from the impact that this explosion had on my mind and body."

From *Autobiography of an Awakening*

The effects of this unexpected, explosive visitation from the unknown left me stunned for days. As is often the case with miraculous and unanticipated events like this, eventually I found myself once again lost in the confusion and ambiguity of a historical and very personal relationship to life. In an individual who is not yet ready to fully respond to the staggering implications of the message given, brief encounters like these slowly settle to the bottom of consciousness, like a broken piece of mirror resting on the ocean floor that casts a faint but glimmering reflection of the light on the surface. Even though I was soon ensconced in the dream of my own life and history once again, that faint but glimmering reflection haunted me in my shallow relationship to life, as it often does for those individuals who have mysteriously stepped beyond the known without having had any clear intention to do so. It took six years of struggle and confusion, during which I remained lost in the morbid condition of identifying principally with my own personal history, to finally bring me to my senses.

Ready to respond at last, I had one intention and one intention only. To liberate myself unconditionally from fear, delusion and ignorance. To free myself from the excruciating state of emotional and psychological slavery that ceaseless meditation on the personal always is. And so I set out on my quest for liberation. I was a sincere seeker only because my intention was clear. But in spite of that, the goal of all spiritual seeking—enlightenment—remained vague and mysterious. This was something I spent a great deal of time trying to locate, figure out and understand. In fact, although I didn't know it at the time, it was to become the very essence of my life. The search for clear answers to difficult and often confusing questions has been and continues to be my passion. This intriguing question—what is the goal of genuine spiritual seeking, what is enlightenment?—continued to perplex and concern me from the very instant that my intention to become free in this life became unconditional.

How is it then that one who is sincere and who truly wants to know can find the answers to the questions: What does enlightenment *look* like and *feel* like? The answers are not as abstract as they may seem. To know what enlightenment *feels* like, the sincere seeker must energetically and one-pointedly pursue the world of spiritual experience.

To know what enlightenment *looks* like, the sincere seeker must closely scrutinize those individuals who seem to have attained that goal themselves. And this is what I did. In order to find out for myself what the goal looked like, I closely observed the character of my teachers. I was seeking for guidance, and did so as many seekers do, through observing and then trying to emulate those qualities in my teachers that attracted me to them in the first place. Hungry for knowledge, I tried to see as many teachers as I could.

Gradually though, over an eight-year period I became doubtful about following a spiritual role model. This was because I had become confused by the discrepancies I observed between the teachings that my teachers gave and the way they lived their own lives. Even though over time these discrepancies began to disturb me more and more, the pursuit of liberation was more important to me than anything else, and because of this I continued to seek guidance from those who had obviously gone farther than I had.

In order to find out what the goal felt like, I experimented with different forms of meditation. The results were very powerful, inspiring and illuminating. I became a serious meditator, rarely missing a day, and was always fascinated and intrigued by the ongoing experience of looking beyond the known. At first I pursued practices of kundalini yoga that promised to reawaken the fullness and splendor of my awakening at sixteen. In fits and starts this did indeed occur, and at times I was even left swooning at the miraculous powers that these practices held. Experiences of powerful energy, bliss and at moments intoxicating love moved me deeply.

Later, inspired by the possibility of diving deep into meditation for weeks at a time, I was exposed to the practice of Buddhist meditation, which to my amazement revealed a very different approach to the goal. The emphasis was on the discovery of emptiness and clarity. Powerful experiences of insight revealed temporarily that the movement of thought was empty or selfless. A new perspective opened up to me: the potential of ultimately becoming free from the tyranny of the mind and the endless identification with memory. Insight into the causes of psychological and emotional suffocation were revealed to me in a new and thrilling way.

I came to a point in my career as a seeker when the seeming differences between these approaches—the experience of fullness as goal and the revelation of emptiness as goal—troubled me. What was the difference between the experience of fullness and the discovery of emptiness? I thought about this question incessantly as I had tasted both experiences and had become confused as to which direction to follow. Even though I took every opportunity I could to ask different teachers this question, it was never answered to my satisfaction. I was at an interesting crossroad in my life because I knew that if I wanted to succeed I needed to put all my eggs in one basket, and yet was unsure which path to pursue wholeheartedly. Also by that time, the strong doubts I had as to whether to rely on any teacher for guidance on the path to final liberation needed to be resolved. The direction I was leaning in was that relying on anyone other than myself could be a great impediment.

It was then that I met a little-known teacher named H.W.L. Poonja in Lucknow in northern India. Miraculously, in a very short time he revealed to me the answers to the two questions that had plagued me. First, his response to my question of fullness versus emptiness as final experience of the goal was simple and direct. He told me that they were ultimately one and the same. Hearing this relieved me of the burden of doubt and confusion that I had been carrying and released the hidden glory of all that had been revealed to me spontaneously fourteen years earlier. Secondly, the expression and manifestation of his character healed the disillusionment of the past. There seemed to be no discrepancy between his teaching and the way he lived his life, and he demonstrated to me in profound ways selfless love, wisdom and compassion.

Chapter 8

DIVERGING PATHS

H.W.L. Poonja's message to me, and to by now countless other seekers who have come to him, is simply this: that all effort and striving to become free is itself the main impediment to the direct realization of the fact that one has never been unfree. His admonishment to drop all effort, struggle and striving to *achieve* liberation had a staggering effect on me, as it has on many others. His example, along with the miracle of my own transformation, initially resulted in a strong confidence that his teaching was absolute and perfect.

Proclaiming me to be his chosen son, the one he had been waiting for all his life, he told me that I had understood everything that he had to teach and that I should devote my life to sharing this message of simple and direct liberation with others. Swept away by the extraordinary events that ensued from our first meeting I had no time to doubt, because as soon as I left his company after only a few brief weeks, this message of simple and direct realization began to pour out of me, often with almost unbearable intensity. The effects were immediate and dramatic. Friends fell into deep meditation in my presence and the message of liberation here and now was constantly streaming from me.

The explosive transmission of this simple yet profound teaching continued unabated and its impact on others continued to astound me. I was in awe most of the time. In Europe, almost overnight many gathered around me, and the intensity of their experience inspired a large number to leave behind their former lives in order to allow nothing to interfere with the miracle of awakening that was revealing itself to them daily. My life had become a living fairy tale with no bumps, scratches or nicks. I was on a magical and mysterious roller coaster ride that screamed perfection.

Slowly though, cracks appeared. The simple yet profound teaching of perfect liberation here and now, for any and all who would be willing to drop all striving and effort to become free, revealed flaws in its ability to address the full range of actual needs of most individuals. The initial discovery of freedom that resulted when individuals let go of all notions of effort and striving was in most, I discovered, only temporary. Whether the initial experience of Self-discovery lasted a few hours or a few weeks, in almost every case I began to find that the old, conditioned and very personal relationship to life as a whole began to surface and reassert its influence once again. Over time it became unavoidably clear that far more was necessary to truly liberate an individual from fear, delusion and ignorance than my guru's simple teaching of letting go of effort. The extraordinary ambivalence of the human condition when faced with the highest possibility of perfect liberation began to reveal itself to me in all its complexity. The depth of identification with false and wrong views about the nature of reality, relative and absolute, demanded far more than mere glimpses into one's ultimate nature to finally liberate the individual from fear, ignorance and self-deception. The human predicament was revealed to me to be a delicate one, and because of this it became more and more obvious that the human condition needed to be met with a teaching that would leave no stone unturned.

As it gradually became apparent that my own teaching was deviating from my guru's in order to meet the needs of those around me, simultaneously I came to the painful discovery of the fact that my guru was not the man he appeared to be. Over time it became clear that in the face of unequivocal declarations of love and perfect union, my guru was demonstrating dishonesty and duplicity. Eventually he would even conspire to undermine my teaching work. The entire story is told in my book *Autobiography of an Awakening*. The issues that eventually led to the ultimate dissolution of our relationship are many and complex. The very nature of the meaning and significance of spiritual awakening has all been brought into question through the painful unfolding of a conflict that reveals the entire panorama of important questions that need to be addressed by any individual who sincerely wants to be free in this life.

Chapter 9

A Crisis of Trust

The Path and the Goal Are One

The genuine pursuit of spiritual liberation is the pursuit of unity and simplicity. Unity is not only the fact of our ultimate nature, but indeed, if there is any significance in spiritual attainment, unity must finally become the very essence of the expression of the individual who claims to have achieved the goal of unity itself. It is my conviction in this, what I consider to be such an obvious point, that has forced me to stand alone in a time when something so obvious seems to be so misunderstood. The meaning and significance of enlightenment to me is, and I truly believe always has been, the final attainment of nonduality, *not only as inner vision but as that expression of singularity and undivided purity of intention that leaves no room for doubt, confusion or ambiguity.*

Simply because I have not wanted to compromise on this matter, I have gained a reputation of being controversial. Unwavering in my insistence that any individual who dares to show the way for others be willing to live up to the highest expression of human potential, I often find myself alone in what seems like a ridiculous predicament. Many misinterpret my motives in speaking about the failings of other teachers, concluding that my intention is simply to find fault. I have found it necessary to do so only because I feel it is essential at this time to try and demystify the aura and mystique of enlightenment. The utter simplicity of the meaning and significance of profound spiritual attainment in the modern world remains largely hidden behind myth and superstition. And therefore, it is only by scrutinizing those who have penetrated deeply into the spiritual dimension, that the common denominator that reveals the important differences and essential similarities of those individuals can be brought to light.

The entire process of spiritual evolution and transformation is, after all, only the search for and attainment of a fully *human* condition. This significant point, while obvious to some, is not so apparent to many. As a matter of fact, in my journeys throughout the world I am always struck by the degree of misinformation that abounds regarding this point. Far too many believe that those individuals who have transcended fear, delusion and ignorance have become no different than living gods. In fact, some of my students were told by a well-known rinpoche that their first mistake was thinking that the Buddha was human! It is precisely this kind of thinking that perpetuates the superstitious beliefs that make any simple yet profound understanding of enlightenment difficult to attain.

Recognizing spiritual evolution and transformation as the struggle for a fully human condition makes it possible for anyone who is sincerely interested to come to an understanding of what real attainment is all about. As long as the meaning and significance of spiritual awakening is allowed to remain so shrouded in mystery, it will continue to seem beyond the reach of most to truly understand. There are many paths but the goal is one. This fact must be clarified in a simple and understandable way. Only then will many of us be able to grow up, and in doing so realize the profound independence that results from seeing clearly through eyes that have been freed from false and wrong views.

A Divided Condition

I never knew until I began to teach how profound is the deeply divided condition of most human beings. And I learned early on how extraordinarily difficult it seems to be for most human beings to express an undivided relationship to life. Indeed, it is the divided condition of the human personality that has for so long created the endless cycle of conflict that has been and continues to be the crux of the spiritual dilemma of the race. Interestingly enough, *it is only when a human being makes that critical decision to find the Truth Absolute, that the depth and complexity of compromise that had been the expression of a divided personality is revealed.* This discovery is often shocking, for few human beings are prepared to come to terms with the enormity of the gap that is exposed between the way one imagines oneself to be and the way one truly is.

A passionate response to the yearning for liberation reveals that a divided condition is entirely *volitional*. In this revelation, the individual discovers for themselves the path to wholeness. That path is the sudden or gradual unwillingness to compromise in matters of the heart and ultimately in one's relationship to what it means to be a fully human being.

It is for this reason that I feel it is so essential that those individuals, who have been fortunate enough to have fallen into the miracle of transcendent spiritual realization, be able to demonstrate an attainment that clearly and unambiguously expresses the evolutionary potential of the race. For as long as this demand is not made, and those who are showing the way for others are allowed to demonstrate the very same schizophrenic condition of contradictory impulses as everyone else, then the attainment of true simplicity and unequivocal victory over ignorance will remain a myth.

The magnitude of the implications inherent in this, what might not seem like such a crucial matter to some, is extraordinary. Without clear examples, the possibility of a collective evolutionary leap is unimaginable. That is why it is so destructive for the evolutionary potential of the race as a whole when those who have realized that transcendental spiritual perspective seem to be unwilling to go all the way.

That possibility can only be sufficiently demonstrated in a personality that is so firmly rooted in the absolute fact of unity that it will only by its nature express that condition unmistakably and unambiguously as itself.

The Need for Clear Examples

The modern spiritual world has been plagued by countless shocking revelations of that vital discrepancy between word and deed. This has created an air of cynicism and a crisis of trust. It should cause the independent thinker to question the ultimate validity of the attainment of those in whom these discrepancies have become painfully obvious. Yet I have been intrigued by the general lack of serious inquiry into this important question.

As long as significant contradiction exists in any individual who is proclaimed to have reached the yonder shore, it's possible that maybe they stopped somewhere short of the beach. I have been surprised at the acceptance and ambivalence in relationship to this matter in seekers and finders alike. This point is crucial and its significance demands some attention in a serious student of evolutionary potential. What makes this matter so confusing to so many is the fact that it is very difficult to ascertain the actual attainment of another as long as one is struggling within the initial stages of awakening oneself. It is because most of those who aspire to final liberation are precisely at that juncture in their own evolution that they usually feel insufficiently evolved to dare to assume such knowledge. This plus the air of cynicism so prevalent in the time we are living in has made it for many a sign of arrogance to question these matters in a passionate way. From early on in my teaching career, I was compelled to do so because I wanted to understand how and why the actual goal of spiritual seeking and practice was so vague, complex and confusing. I found out almost from the very beginning that this kind of questioning was not generally appreciated, and more often than not was scorned, if not outright condemned.

I have always encouraged others to ask themselves the same questions that I have asked myself, and have discovered that few seem to be deeply interested in asking the kinds of questions that challenge the very foundations of our spiritual beliefs. So often the need to cling onto experiences long gone, beliefs based on superstition and if nothing else only hope seems more important to far too many than the pursuit of the Truth unadorned. Many seekers choose to lazily accept that which cannot bear too much scrutiny for fear of ultimately having to scrutinize themselves far too closely.

Endeavoring to rouse from slumber those insisting that a promise unfulfilled was other than that, I have tried to encourage honest inquiry.

Shortly before the demise of my relationship with my own teacher, I was attending one of his teachings with a small group of my students. When they asked him about the discrepancy between the word and deed of well-known spiritual teachers he became irritated, replying that questions such as these have nothing to do with liberation but only with religion. Indeed, in his own philosophy there is not necessarily any relationship between the realization of our true nature and the manifestation of the human personality of the one who has realized it.

In Boulder, Colorado I spoke to a gathering in which some disciples of the late Trungpa Rinpoche were present. When I simply stated what everyone already knew, that his abuse of alcohol had killed him and had led some of his followers to become members of Alcoholics Anonymous, many were offended. Who was I to judge?

Several years after the death of the legendary Bhagwan Rajneesh, I continue to find that most of his devotees are still unable to even begin to contemplate the possibility that their guru might have had something to do with the treacherous escapades of some of his closest disciples.

During a radio interview in Amsterdam by a woman who was a devotee of the late Swami Muktananda, I mentioned the widely known fact that he had gone to bed with the young daughters of his own disciples whom he had asked to be celibate. She was outraged.

In so many cases, discipleship unknowingly becomes a form of spiritual slavery. Too many are unwilling to question the perfection of the attainment of their teacher for fear of threatening the perceived link with the absolute that the teacher represents.

The spiritual crisis of the human race is a crisis of trust. For awakened perception to become stable and permanent, the individual must find a way to trust that is above and beyond the usual perimeters of human experience. It is the inability and unwillingness to trust that makes the goal of utter simplicity and perfect union seem so distant. Indeed, trust is the very foundation of spiritual transformation.

The integrity and inherent perfection of life is demonstrated in that individual who has deeply realized and is able to manifest unity and simplicity. That is why the significance of some individuals actually being able to demonstrate that attainment as self unambiguously is so great. The explosive and deeply liberating power of trust can only manifest itself in that spiritual arena where no taint of ambiguity about the living reality of that possibility exists. As long as any doubt, gross or subtle, continues to exist, it will be almost impossible for the individual to trust in the possibility of realizing their *own* potential as a fully human being.

THE
MODERN SPIRITUAL
PREDICAMENT

Chapter 10

THE MODERN
SPIRITUAL PREDICAMENT

I was born in 1955 so I missed much of the excitement experienced by so many during the psychedelic revolution. That revolution revealed unimaginable possibilities that shook the very foundation of fundamental beliefs people had about what was possible. Through the ingestion of miraculous, mind-altering substances, many individuals realized literally overnight that their perspective had been shockingly limited. In light of this newly discovered perspective, the necessity of completely reevaluating all prior assumptions and conclusions about what was true and what was important became obvious. A veil had been lifted, and for many it was no longer possible to carry on in the old way.

But it soon became apparent that the mere ingestion of psychedelic drugs was not enough to truly transform. And so the pilgrimage to the East began. Many were in search of ways and means to fulfill the promise of transformation revealed in the psychedelic experience and sought wisdom and guidance from the ancient teachings of Hinduism,

Buddhism and Taoism. Various teachings, teachers and practices of all kinds were pursued in earnest and the results were often dramatic and inspiring. Soon seekers were returning from the East with tales of remarkable meetings with extraordinary people. They also proclaimed that through the pursuit of various spiritual practices, there was now a way to actualize the transformation the potential of which had been discovered in the experiment with psychedelics. Eastern teachers were invited to the West and soon westerners who had studied in Asia also began to teach. The same excitement generated by the use of psychedelics was now experienced by those who turned to eastern spiritual practices. Previously unimaginable possibilities actually did seem in reach and a movement began in the West based on the conviction that a radical transformation in consciousness could occur.

It was only when I began to teach in 1986 that I started to become aware of the fact that for the most part the promise had not been fulfilled. I discovered that many of those whom I had looked up to as a seeker had over time, without realizing it, become cynical about the possibility of radical transformation. The reasons for this I think were twofold. Too many masters from the East had lost their mystique of perfection through corruption and scandal. Also it seemed that many of the practices that had promised enlightenment were not producing the results that had been anticipated.

It has been a constant revelation to me how little faith many of the original western messengers of freedom now have in the possibility of truly radical transformation. To me it has seemed for some time now that in many the innocence that is a prerequisite for genuine enlightenment has been lost. For the quantum leap to occur, the individual must believe without any doubt that radical transformation is an actual possibility. To believe that such a leap is possible, an innocence that is uncorrupted by cynicism or fear must be found. Indeed, most human beings can only bear to sustain this kind of profound vulnerability for very brief periods of time. Without the illusion of security that fixed conclusions about what is possible provide, most individuals experience terror and an unbearable sense of insecurity. To avoid this condition of undefended receptivity, most hide behind cynical views and fixed conclusions that protect them from the overwhelming insecurity of daring to believe in a life with no boundaries.

I come from the second generation of modern western spiritual practitioners in pursuit of enlightenment, and my own experience has forced me to question many of the prevailing ideas that have become status quo in the contemporary spiritual world. It seems that twenty or thirty years later, many of those who in their youthful idealism seemed willing to take enormous risks in order to fulfill the promise of the transcendental vision have over time become willing to settle for compromise. Many give lip service to the need for extraordinary transformation, but the kind of lives that so many spiritual people seem willing to accept tends to make me wonder. The idealistic insistence on the need to question all prior assumptions and conclusions about that which is true and important has been replaced by a willingness to accept many of the very structures that at one time were revealed to be flawed. Intense passion about spiritual possibilities is often reduced to mere naive idealism by many of those who once experienced a similar conviction.

The fact is that very few of those who aspired to the highest heights of spiritual attainment have penetrated beyond the superficial layers of spiritual insight and experience. Those few from the East and the West who have, have often betrayed the depth of their own attainment through succumbing to the temptations of lust and greed for power. Ironically, those who have gone the farthest and who could have made the deepest impression have, through their own failings, helped to create the prevailing mood of cynicism that they could have destroyed.

It is only through clear examples that the entire status quo of cynical convictions can be ultimately challenged. And it is only through the discovery of profound vulnerability and undefended receptivity that one would dare to believe in the possibility of unconditional transformation.

Chapter 11

MEETING THE STATUS QUO

The Meditation Teacher

When I had been teaching for only six months, I was invited to dinner by an American meditation teacher whom I had known in my days as a seeker. He was looking forward to our meeting because he wanted to see for himself what had happened to me. Soon after I sat down, he began to ask me questions about my experience. I repeatedly said that it would be better to wait until after we had eaten, as I sensed something uncontrollable might happen if we began to speak in a serious way. He found this difficult to understand.

After we had finished dinner, we sat down in chairs opposite each other and he proceeded to question me about my experience. Almost immediately I was overwhelmed with ecstasy, and simultaneously I felt all barriers of time, space and personal identity fall away. My answers and the power and intensity with which they were pouring out of me shocked my host. Engulfed by the unknown, all prior assumptions about who I was were rendered irrelevant, and therefore it became impossible for me to be anything but utterly real. My laughter echoed a knowing confidence that could not pretend otherwise. When I said that all the books on his bookshelf were useless if he truly wanted to be free, his expression changed from shock to anger. When I said that I was sitting before him completely naked and that I meant no disrespect, he seemed to withdraw even more.

The room was filled with a powerful presence and my friend seemed at a loss to comprehend what was occurring. He concluded only that I had become arrogant, and I suspect also felt I had lost my mind. I had, but he was unable to appreciate how fortunate I was to have done so. Eight years later, he is still teaching other people how to meditate.

A Spiritual Community

A significant number of those who were coming to see me when I began to teach in England were part of a meditation community that had been loosely associated for over ten years. In the early 1980s, I had been a student of the leader of that community. Many in the group had spent several years in India in the 1970s practicing meditation intensively. At that time, most had abandoned worldly ambitions for the promise of enlightenment. When I came on the scene in the second half of the 1980s, I discovered that many of these people had long ago given up on that promise and were now, to my surprise, almost all immersed in different forms of psychotherapy. This intrigued me as I had heard about these individuals over the years of my own seeking and had looked up to many of them. Suddenly I found myself in the unusual position of teaching those who had been at it far longer than I had.

Within a few weeks of my arrival, most of the core group found themselves on fire with the passion for liberation once again. When they had all met in India years earlier, their intention was only to become free, to be enlightened in this birth and to be able to manifest that enlightenment in a profound and extraordinary way. That which most had long since abandoned hope for was now burning in their veins. It was then that I began to have intimations of what the future might bring. I watched in amazement as ideas that had become fixed about what was possible crumbled. Innocence and passion rediscovered created an air of excitement and renewed willingness to take risks. Within a few months almost all of the members of the board of their meditation center had decided to leave, not only because they were admitting their disillusionment, but because they had found what they had originally been looking for. Their western teachers, whom they had met in India and began their journey with years earlier, were not pleased. In fact, when they tried to speak to them about their experience, to their surprise, their enthusiasm was met with disinterest.

Later, the leader of the community commented, "The problem with Andrew was that he was only interested in enlightenment. He never wanted to settle into the practice."

The Hospice Worker

In 1987 when I was teaching in Amsterdam, a man in his early forties came from America to see me. He had originally been inspired by Ram Dass. His spiritual journey eventually led him to Asia where he became a Buddhist monk for some time. Later he traveled throughout India, meditating and visiting different spiritual teachers. When I met him, he had long since disrobed and had become a hospice worker, running a center that helped people face into and prepare for their own death. He also led meditation retreats. He came to me because he said he wanted to be free.

One morning, bubbling with joy and excitement he came to visit me, proclaiming, "I want to bring you to the States to teach. I want to introduce you to all my friends."

Six months later I was on my way to America, he having prepared the way. When I arrived, he stayed with my wife and me and a small group of other students in a large house in the country. But something had changed. The joy and excitement was gone and he looked terrible. He told me he was terrified of letting go. He said, disappointed in himself, "I'm unable to trust." Soon after, he was gone.

He returned to his hospice work, and within days he was once again helping people face into their own death and teaching others how to meditate.

The Transpersonal Psychologist

Shortly after I moved back to America, I lived and taught in western Massachusetts for six months. A woman in her early fifties came to see me teach almost every night for three weeks. She was a therapist, a teacher and trainer of transpersonal psychologists, and a Buddhist who had practiced meditation for years. From the very first evening she came, she was intrigued. She had many questions and we often spoke at great length. One night she asked me, "Andrew, how do you do it? You're able to get people to let go in such a short time. In my work this usually takes years. I'm fascinated by how well you know people and how deeply you're able to work with each person. Just watching it is wonderful."

After a few weeks something interesting happened. Instead of being the observer, she became the observed. Unexpectedly she now found herself the object of attention, because this time she was the one on the spot. Seeing that she was not able to let go, she looked at me and smiled knowingly. "My number is up," she said.

The next day, she left to teach a training course for transpersonal psychologists. A week later I received a card from her which said, "I haven't run away. I want you to know I still want to be free." I never saw her again.

Chapter 12

It's Black or White

Ever since the very beginning of my teaching career, people have responded to my message in extreme ways. I have always been passionate as a teacher, not due to any choice of my own. Compelled by a knowing that streams up from deep inside of me, I am often as surprised as anyone else at how strongly I feel about the need to awaken. To some this passion has given great courage and inspiration; to others it has caused aversion and even offense. Initially this struck me as odd, as I have always only spoken about the possibility of becoming truly free in *this* life, and about being willing to sacrifice any and all obstacles for that end. While this made perfect sense to many, others found it extreme. My insistence that a seeker's relationship to spiritual liberation was ultimately black or white, yes or no, was often not well received. This approach was perceived as being too absolute. Over time I began to understand why. It became clear that this teaching left little room for the individual who was not convinced that they wanted to go all the way.

As I met more and more seekers, many of whom had already been on the path for some time, it became apparent that for the most part they were trying to fit the explosive revelation of enlightenment into a life that was based on very personal and fundamentally limited motives. It was rare that even those who were lucky enough to have glimpsed the enlightened perspective were able to ultimately break free from the confines of a personal and historical relationship to life. It became obvious that unless the seeker had the intention of unconditionally liberating themselves from the veil of the personal, no matter how deeply they dove into the unknown, they would almost always return to a view that was profoundly limited. Indeed, it seemed that most seekers, without realizing it, were trying to fit that which had no limit into a shell that could never contain it.

I began to understand why so few had gotten very far. So much of what was being pursued in the name of spiritual awakening seemed merely to romanticize and glorify a perspective that was fundamentally limited, rather than completely obliterating it so that a new perspective untainted by the needs of the personal could reveal itself. As long as the individual has any investment in that which is personal, their ability to interpret the way discovered in profound revelation will always be distorted by that need. It is impossible to contain the explosive and ultimately revolutionary implications of the spiritual vision as long as the individual feels compelled to hold on in any way to that which is old, safe or known.

THE DISCOVERY
OF A BIGGER VIEW

Chapter 13

THE DISCOVERY OF
A BIGGER VIEW

My own search for liberation was, as it is for most people, focused on myself. The larger implications of awakening were for the most part not in the foreground of my consciousness. I wanted to attain final liberation from fear and insecurity, and more than that, I wanted to become convinced beyond any trace of doubt, as I had been once before, that my existence was in no way separate from all of life. When miraculously in a few short weeks with my teacher this indeed did occur, I was shocked. This shock increased by leaps and bounds in the ensuing weeks when, to my amazement, this same event—the miracle of Self-discovery—began to occur in those around me. But soon, shock grew into fascination when I began to observe something even more miraculous than the moment of Self-discovery, which was the dissolution of boundaries between those in whom the Self had been discovered. The ecstasy of perfect intimacy and absolute trust revealed a freedom of being that gradually became more significant than the liberation of any individual.

In the first few years of my teaching career, my emphasis was still on the liberation of the individual alone, but I couldn't help but continue to be aware of the fact that something far more important was occurring. Those who gathered around me seemed to be sharing a view which eventually proved itself to be far more important than the experience of any individual. That view was that there is no other.

The ecstasy of communion first became apparent to me shortly after I began teaching. At that time I had been living for two months with seven other people in Rishikesh in northern India. As we spent our days and nights together immersed in the bliss of Self-discovery, the mystery of the timeless that was being shared was like an energy field that seemed to surround us. Being together was being alone, and in that aloneness there was nowhere else to go. It seemed that through being together the illusion of individuality became even more apparent. The boundaries between inner and outer literally had dissolved—it was often difficult to know where one ended and the other began.

Shortly thereafter I was invited to England and within a few weeks people started gathering together to hear the teaching. Even though I was still, in the way I had been taught, emphasizing liberation of the individual alone, the people who were gathering around me seemed to be experiencing liberation not only through spending time with me, but through simply being together.

A few months later I moved to Holland. It was then that I knew beyond any doubt that the significance of what was being shared by those individuals who had come to me far transcended the motives that I or any of them originally had. The original motive that I had as a teacher was to liberate the individual. The motive that many of those who came to me originally had was to find freedom for themselves. Now we all found ourselves in the midst of something else altogether. We were swimming in an ocean of being where it became clear that what was revealing itself spontaneously through the collective consciousness was the evolutionary potential of the race as a whole.

Accepting the Larger Implications

After two years in Europe I moved to Massachusetts. Many people chose to follow me there and I soon found myself in an interesting predicament. I realized that I now had to come to terms with the fact that what was occurring around me was in substance far different than what I had been taught and what I initially thought that I was teaching. Enlightenment that transcended liberation for the individual alone was manifesting itself clearly in front of my eyes, and that fact now needed to be addressed by me and those around me.

What were the implications of this event that was unfolding and that was taking a direction other than even I had originally been aware of? They seemed to be many and far reaching, and above all of the utmost significance to each and every individual involved.

We found ourselves coming together in such a way that the experience of the individual appeared to be less important than the collective context in which that experience occurred. That context was one of perfect and unbroken unity in the realization of one Self. It appeared that precisely because of that context the impulse to evolve could express itself in a rare and remarkable way. The collective consciousness itself seemed to demand that all the individuals involved rise up to a higher level of being. What was extraordinary to behold was the birth of a spiritual conscience in the group as a whole that was able to see and feel with greater depth than many of the individuals on their own. Indeed, being together in this way the intrusive presence of ego became glaringly obvious not just to some individuals, but to the collective consciousness of the group as a whole. Any need to remain separate that stemmed from the fear of that unity became apparent in a stark yet potentially liberating way. It became easier for those individuals who sincerely wanted to be free to become undeniably aware of exactly what it was that had always been obscuring that freedom. And even more importantly, the birth of that context revealed the way to perfect transcendence literally and unambiguously, not only for one but for all to see.

True liberation became no longer a distant possibility, but a living potential for any individual who had the courage to let go. And even more significant was the fact that the simultaneous recognition of unity by so many revealed a thrilling evolutionary potential. It seemed to call each and every one of those who were aware of it to leave behind any and all obstructions to that unity so that the fact of oneness could become manifest in this world, not only as inner knowing by one but as objective fact by many. Indeed, it seemed that heaven could become manifest on earth if only a few were willing.

The bond of love and mystical communion that had drawn us together was making apparent the fact that conformity by the individuals involved to the demand of a higher principle was essential.

Too often the experience of mystical union remains only a revelation of the extraordinary evolutionary potential inherent in the human condition. When the shadow normally cast by the ego temporarily dissolves, the light of the living Truth unobscured reveals not only the glorious and inherent perfection of life, but even more importantly the *way* that that perfection can become manifest in a seemingly imperfect world. When the way is revealed, all things become possible. But that possibility is rarely actualized, and when it is, it usually remains limited to one individual alone. Unless the spiritual vision is able to manifest itself beyond the individual, the profound evolutionary potential inherent in that vision cannot truly unfold.

Chapter 14

FOR THE SAKE OF THE WHOLE

Through the intensity of being together in the kind of intimacy that was constantly being shared, the fact of the impersonal nature of the entire experience of human life became more and more obvious. The evolutionary significance of enlightenment for the race as a whole had to now be given preference over the belief that enlightenment was strictly a personal matter. As those around me began to acknowledge this shift in emphasis from the personal to the larger or more impersonal nature of enlightenment, an important question arose. What is the meaning of personal freedom within the context of an impersonal perspective?

The desire for personal freedom divorced from the evolutionary implications of enlightenment revealed in the vast, impersonal view became meaningless. It became meaningless because in light of the perspective of the ultimately impersonal implications of enlightenment itself, the individual could no longer ignore the inherent responsibility that they held for the race as a whole.

Indeed, the discovery of the impersonal perspective made apparent that the desire to awaken itself could never only be a personal matter. That discovery revealed to the individual that it was imperative to awaken not only for their own sake but for the sake of the whole; because in the direct realization of the nondifference between self and other, that responsibility could no longer be avoided.

The discovery of the responsibility realized in the transcendent spiritual vision is usually what is immediately forgotten when the intensity of short-term immersion in the ocean of being diminishes. The individual who is fundamentally concerned with themselves tends to almost always avoid the overwhelming implications of the discovery that they are not separate from the whole. The burden that the weight of this realization casts on the personality is excruciating for any individual who is still in any way attached to and identified with even a trace of personal history. It is difficult, if not impossible, to preserve that which sees itself as being separate while allowing the attention to expand without limitation.

The need to preserve any notion of individuality will always cast a long shadow, and that shadow will always distort the reflection of the world of time and space on the mirror of perception. I am continuously fascinated by the myriad ways in which the shadow of individuality creates a distorted reflection, thereby making it so difficult for most individuals to see things as they actually are. The most fundamental manifestation of ignorance is the inability to see things as they are; and the reason why human beings have so consistently found it so difficult to come together in an extraordinary way is precisely because of the distortion in perception that is created when attention is distracted by the need to preserve false notions of self.

Indeed, when two individuals come together, conflict becomes inevitable as long as both remain deeply distracted by the need to preserve false and wrong notions of self. In order for a final attainment of the way to become stable in any individual, remaining free from all false notions of self is vital. When coming together has been recognized as being essential for transcendent realization to become manifest beyond the personal, the need to remain free from all false notions of self becomes even more vital.

Chapter 15

RIGHT VIEW IS THE DISCOVERY OF THE HOLY GRAIL

The path and the goal are one. The goal is the attainment of right view. Right view is the discovery of the holy grail. The holy grail is the discovery of that immaculate perception or view in which the true and right relationship of all things is revealed. Right view is that perspective of reality in which the true and right relationship of all things is directly perceived. Direct perception of the true and right relationship of all things is the goal and the way.

As long as the mirror of perception is tainted by even one speck of dust, right view has not been attained. Right view is that clear reflection of actuality that always perfectly reveals the way between all pairs of opposites. A perfect response is always born from the unbroken abidance in that view that is free from distortion. *The attainment of that view that makes a perfect response constant and inevitable is the goal of final liberation.*

The holy grail is that right view from which the ultimate truth of nonseparation can become manifest clearly and unambiguously in the world of time and space. Perfect response, which is the natural expression of the attainment of right view, is the explosive demonstration of evolutionary potential inherent in the fully human condition. The ability to respond perfectly alone makes all things possible. In that perfect response, heaven can and does become manifest on earth.

For the evolutionary leap to occur en masse in the human race, the attainment of right view is essential. Without it, any and all attempts to manifest heaven on earth, no matter how well intentioned, can never truly succeed.

THE VISCERAL
RESPONSE

Chapter 16

THE ZEN MASTER AND THE YOGI

In my ongoing interest in deepening my understanding of the awakened condition, I have taken every opportunity to meet spiritual teachers from different traditions. This has been and continues to be a fascinating and educational experience. It is far too easy to assume that we have come farther than we actually have if we are not willing to test the depth and validity of our own conclusions. It is only through making the effort to seek out the company of those who seem to have the same depth of interest in liberation of the human spirit as we do, that we will be given the opportunity to test our own knowledge and find out if there are any limitations in our own view. So often teacher and student alike too easily become self-satisfied and over-confident in the belief that their path and their way is perfect and beyond question. The spiritual path is the search for and discovery of total insecurity. More often than not, it becomes the very opposite of that.

The validity of any teacher, path or system can only

ultimately be determined by their results. The result, rather than the promise, is what I have always been interested in. Often what can seem to be a perfect teacher, teaching or tradition can, when scrutinized more closely, be discovered to be far from that.

If one peers deeply into the human condition when faced with the highest possibility of perfect liberation, one tends to find more questions than answers.

Two years into my teaching career, a man in his early fifties who had been on the spiritual path for more than half his life came to see me. I was particularly intrigued when he told me that he had been a student of a renowned Zen master under whose tutelage he had participated in fifty sesshins. Having done some Buddhist practice myself, I had heard much about the strength of will and stamina necessary to do these arduous meditation retreats. They were, it seemed, the most rigorous and demanding form of intensive practice that one could do. I was interested in this man's experience not only because of how much practice he had done, but also because I had heard so much about the Zen master under whose guidance he had studied. A teacher of tremendous energy, he was known for tirelessly traversing the planet, teaching one sesshin after another. I had heard from others who had done sesshins with him that he was a very demanding teacher while at the same time very compassionate. When several years later the man who had come to see me, now my student, had offered to arrange a meeting with the Roshi, I was thrilled. He was reputed to be the greatest living Zen master in America.

On a beautiful fall day I went with three of my students to meet him at his retreat center in the desert outside of Los Angeles. When I first saw him, I was struck by his beautiful face and the strength and power that seemed to emanate from his extremely small body. His serenity and quiet confidence were the unmistakable mark of one who has found himself and who is no longer afraid of life.

I began our meeting by saying that I was amazed by how much confusion and corruption there was in the modern spiritual world. He seemed surprised by this and responded by saying that if dismay was the basis of my teaching then there was ego. I said that the basis of my teaching was love. I remember at the time not understanding his point, but thought to myself that eventually it would become clear to me. Later I went on to describe the foundation of my teaching. I said if one wanted to be free, it was imperative that one find a way to take no position in relationship to all thought, feeling and experience. At the same time, I went on to say, one must come to terms with the paradoxical fact that as we are human beings and we have to act, we can't avoid taking a position in relationship to thought, feeling and experience. He liked what I said, but stated that this shouldn't be only intellectual. I said my understanding was the result of the investigation of love. "Good," he said. "To have a following, one must be a true lover and be able to show that the Source is the same Source of student, teacher and ant."

There was a warm feeling between us and the atmosphere was one of respect and seriousness. We spent over an hour together with several of my own students and his in attendance. When I spoke about the passion I felt burning inside me to awaken others and about the revolutionary implications of enlightenment, he said he supported me, but cautioned me not to be too flurried in my passion. He told me that some will agree with me and some will not, but all are my friends. He impressed me more by his presence and unusually natural condition than by what he said. Often the communication was difficult because not only were we speaking through a translator, but also many of his responses took the form of Zen aphorisms, some of which I found difficult to understand.

In the car on the way back to Los Angeles, the translator, an American who had been a longtime student of the Roshi, explained to us in great depth and detail his understanding of the Roshi's teaching, which made it even more apparent that he was a man of high attainment. Pleased by our meeting, I looked forward to the opportunity of speaking with the Roshi a second time in greater depth. I thought about what the Roshi had said to me, that my dismay at the modern spiritual predicament could be a sign of ego. I thought about this deeply and always found myself unable to understand what he was getting at. My confusion about this matter deepened even more several months later when one of my students spoke to his chief disciple in Vienna about our meeting. Apparently when his disciple asked the Roshi what he had thought of me, he responded by saying he thought I was crazy. I was perplexed as this seemed like an extreme response to what appeared to have been a respectful and warm exchange. I wondered about what it was that I could have said or done that would cause such a response from one who seemed to have gone so far.

Several months later while I was teaching in New York City, I found out. A man who came to hear me speak had read an article written by the student who had introduced me to the Roshi. He said that the article which described the Roshi as a man of integrity had, it seemed, portrayed him very inaccurately. He went on to say that a close friend of his had been sexually abused by the Roshi during a private interview at a sesshin. Apparently she had been so disturbed by this event that it took her several years to recover. Since that time, more stories about other escapades of the Roshi reached me. So it was not then difficult to understand why the Roshi cautioned me about my passion and felt that my objection to corruption was the expression of ego.

When I was teaching in Santa Fe, New Mexico I noticed that a western man with a long beard who was wearing a white turban was listening to me with rapt attention. At the end of the evening, he asked to speak with me privately. Later when we spoke, he told me he was one of the chief disciples of a famous Indian yogi who had a large community of followers in America and in Europe. I had heard a lot about his guru over the years as he was quite famous. He was a Sikh and all of his western devotees also became Sikhs when they joined his community. Both men and women wore turbans and dressed in white. He had many centers where a rigorous form of yoga and pranayama were taught. His disciple told me that he had been the head of one of his guru's ashrams for many years. He said he very much liked my teaching and then invited me to meet his guru.

The following day, I went to meet him with four of my students. As we approached his residence, we had to stop at the gate where a female armed guard sat in a small room with four windows. As we entered, we were warmly greeted by his disciple who had invited us, along with another disciple who welcomed us with equal warmth. I noticed that both shook my hand with the same strength and assurance. As we walked toward their guru's residence, we passed his fleet of cars which included a Rolls Royce and two Lincoln Continentals that were lined up side by side. Upon entering his house, we were welcomed by several turbaned women and the enticing smell of Indian food being prepared for our lunch. His disciple led my students and me into the living room where he introduced me to his guru. He was a large man whose overweight body was draped over a reclining chair, his legs extended in front of him supported by a footrest. Immediately he said, "Now that he's come, we will stop speaking about business and will speak only about spiritual matters."

I sat in the chair opposite him. It was obvious that he was a very powerful man as he effortlessly commanded the attention of all those around him. As we spoke he looked at me very directly while continuously doing different things with his hands, one minute stroking his long grey beard, another rustling through papers on a small side table next to his chair. Many of the women who had been working in the kitchen came in and sat down. One of them, a middle-aged Indian woman, was his wife. In a short time the atmosphere became quite charged with intensity and a current seemed to fill the room.

Soon after we started speaking, I described to him how I stressed to my students the necessity of being deadly serious about spiritual life, and went on to speak about the confused state of affairs in the modern spiritual world. I said that it was important in the time we are living in that some be willing to set a standard. He responded by saying that everyone goes their own way, and then spoke about the role of karma and destiny. At one point he laughed and said I was too idealistic. "It is a very dangerous thing to be an example for others," he said. "One who is doing so is setting themselves up for a fall." I went on to describe how the example that many teachers were setting was creating an enormous amount of cynicism and doubt about the possibility of purity at a time when it was so sorely needed. He made no bones about the fact that he disagreed with me about this. "In this, I have no choice," I said. To my surprise, he smiled and said, "Yes, I know you have no choice. I can see this is your destiny." Then he turned to his disciples and said, "Look, even when he's being challenged his aura doesn't change." He seemed pleased and we both smiled.

He went on to tell me many stories about himself, about his early life and struggles, and also spoke about one of his teachers. He didn't appear to me to be a man who was enlightened, but at the same time he was undoubtedly very powerful and seemed to possess psychic abilities. At one point, he got a long distance phone call and paused to take care of some business dealings. Then he spoke for a long time, like many Indian teachers do, in a rambling way—one moment quoting scripture, the next telling a story and then speaking in metaphor. In spite of the fact that we obviously disagreed on many fundamental points, the tone of our meeting always remained one of friendship and respect. Although I felt he was a man whom it might be dangerous to trust, he appeared to be sweet and caring. His disciples' love and devotion to him was extraordinary.

We were treated to a sumptuous blend of Indian and Mexican food. After we ate, he made predictions about my future, saying I would be a successful and influential teacher with many students. Then he took a pencil and paper and spent several minutes scribbling numbers. He was an expert on astrology and numerology. He said that my first seven years of teaching were going to be the most difficult and that in one year my hardest times would be over. He spoke to me in a fatherly way and said more than once that I must be protected at all times, even to the degree that when I travel five men should surround me "like a sandwich." He also said that I travel too much and that it was traveling that had ruined his own body. When he found out my wife was Indian and also from a Sikh background, he and his wife both insisted that she come for lunch the following day.

When we left, his disciple walked us to our car. After I thanked him, he looked at me with intense sincerity and said, "Guruji likes you very much and he wanted you to know that if there is anything, anything at all he can do to help you, don't hesitate to ask." As we drove past the armed guard at the gate, I couldn't help but wonder what he meant.

Chapter 17

THE VISCERAL RESPONSE

Shortly after I moved to northern California in the spring of 1989 with one hundred and fifty students, it began to dawn on me that what I was teaching was not for everybody. My constant emphasis on the necessity to put the call of the spiritual life and its demands above and beyond anything else if one truly wanted to be free in this life, I soon found was too great for most seekers. In California, the shocking degree of compromise that has become the status quo in the modern spiritual world hit me like never before. What had been a naive assumption on my part, that most seekers were true seekers—that means clearly understanding the price that had to be paid by any man or woman who wanted to win true spiritual freedom in this life—was soon shattered. The fact that very few seekers and meditators rarely took seriously the possibility of going all the way, made life for one such as myself who teaches nothing else quite challenging. It gradually became clear to me that for the vast majority of seekers, spiritual life provided merely an escape from the mundane, and for others even a form of entertainment. I began to realize that such a call—the call to go all the way—fueled by an enthusiastic willingness to give up anything in order to succeed struck far too deep into the solar plexus of many.

The call to liberation is an impersonal one. It is a call from the Absolute. A beckoning from the Self to the self. When that call is heard directly, even if only for a split second, uncensored by fear or time, in that second one knows everything. One recognizes, even if only for that brief instant, that only *that* is real and all else false. In that realization comes the understanding that attachment to and investment in that which has been recognized as being false, impermanent and unreal is ignorance, and causes bondage, suffering and potentially endless stagnation. But alas, the vision of unending liberation, that vast expanse without beginning or end, poses too great a threat for the majority of seekers who still remain attached to the mirage of selfhood, and who more often than not choose to create the illusion of movement through gradually approaching no limitation by slow and always calculated incremental steps.

The call to awaken from the Self to the self *is* absolute by its very nature. How could it be otherwise? Those who are pure of heart, when recognizing this fact, do not object. But those whose investment in this world is still great experience the call of the Absolute as the ultimate threat to all that has come before and all that they hope will be in the future. The response to the uncompromising nature of the call from the Absolute in the individual who is still attached to this life is experienced as a deep, visceral NO!

As the community of students who had gathered around me gradually began to take on form and structure in order to more efficiently meet the needs of those involved, the mystery of the human condition in all its extreme contradictions became more and more apparent. So much of spiritual life and practice seemed to boil down to being simply that perennial battle between light and darkness, good and evil, heaven and hell. The hellish world of never-ending compromise, where the majority of seekers seemed to be willing to rest for eternity if unchallenged, became recognized as being the status quo of the human condition that had to be taken on wholeheartedly if there was going to be any real chance for a transformation that would be truly revolutionary. Many of my own students, recognizing that a division still existed within them in spite of having experienced a deep penetration into the Absolute, consciously began to embrace a life of renunciation. Endeavoring to face into and come to terms with that division, which was recognized as being the essence of the spiritual predicament, they chose to give up the world for that end alone.

The joy experienced when giving spiritual evolution the highest priority is extraordinary. Allowing oneself to embrace a life without compromise and free from pre-tense is utterly liberating in its depth and singularity. Like none other, it enables the individual to give their full and undivided attention to the destruction of all that is false, wrong and untrue. The individual who has taken the bold step of leaving the world and all the compromise that it represents behind in order to completely and irrevocably destroy the very seeds of that compromise in themselves, when successful often becomes the enemy of the source of that compromise. The source of that compromise is, in the collective/individual mind, a fundamental and deeply existential fear of dissolution, nonexistence and insignificance. It represents an absolute and final loss of freedom for the false and limited notion of self. This fear, which usually remains unconscious and unquestioned, causes the individual to blindly adhere to fixed notions about the nature of reality, including shallow and destructive notions of a personal self that almost always serve to create a world where profound evolution becomes impossible and the law of the spirit is one of stagnation.

The modern spiritual world is in many ways in a similar condition. In spite of the fact that more and more people seem to be expressing interest in the spiritual dimension of life, the deeper layers of the fundamental attachment to time and history usually remain largely untouched. Most revealing about the time we are living in is that even now, when one dares to consider without reservation the deepest implications of the uncompromising call of the Absolute, they often become suspect in the minds of many. But when one not only considers the implications of that call but dares to respond to it unconditionally, thereby stepping outside the collective norm, one is often viewed with suspicion, fear and sometimes even hatred not only by society at large but also by those who profess deep interest in the spiritual life themselves.

It was during those first two years in California that I not only discovered how superficial was the degree of seriousness of many seekers after Truth, but it was then that I began to realize for the first time how deeply conservative and fearful of real change were many of those spiritual practitioners who, now well into their middle age, had been at it for quite a long time. Several of those who were considered quite radical in their own time now seemed to have settled into an alternative lifestyle that appeared a lot more progressive than closer scrutiny would reveal. It seemed to me that many of the old-timers thought they had already been through it all, and therefore had already taken all the big risks and had learned almost everything there was to know. By then most had become therapists or teachers of one kind or another. What was ironic was they were now setting the standard for the masses, many of whom were coming to spiritual life for the first time. But what kind of standard were they setting? They had become the establishment, so to speak, and were at least in my mind stuck in fixed views and conclusions about what was possible and what was true. This made it almost impossible to question fundamental ideas in any way that threatened the status quo that they had over time collectively established. This had become more and more apparent to me since I began teaching when, to my amazement, many of the old-timers expressed dismay, fear and shock when those who came to me became so inspired that they chose to abandon the world to embrace spiritual life wholeheartedly. It was the degree of conviction and the willingness to back it up by taking big risks that seemed to cause the most concern in many who at one time would have been equally thrilled. Indeed several of my students had been Buddhist monks at one time, and interestingly enough when their old friends learned about their newfound degree of conviction and enthusiastic willingness to take big risks once again, the response was one of fear, suspicion and doubt. In a time when so many had given up on the real possibility of extraordinary success, their excitement was seen as naive and even dangerous.

I was intrigued to find that for many whose youth had been characterized by a deep and seemingly sincere questioning of fundamental values and principles, it seemed now that too much of their adult lives were concerned with the search for satisfying intimacy in sexual/romantic relationships and the striving for maturity through becoming parents. The spiritual status quo of the time we are living in shies away from extremes for fear of making the same mistakes that many have made in the recent past—either by becoming too intimately involved with charismatic and too often corrupt spiritual leaders, or by allowing oneself to take the call of the Absolute so seriously that one would begin to neglect more worldly concerns in such a way that would be considered irresponsible. While this is easily understandable, unless one is willing to continue to take big risks until final and irrevocable success has been achieved, the inevitable result will be that like it or not, one will remain in the grips of delusion manifesting itself as the experience of isolation and separation in what is rapidly becoming an overcrowded world. Although many continue to speak passionately about the necessity for radical trans-formation, the unstated law of the land still appears to be every man for himself. When and until the primitive need to live this life for oneself only has been transcended, no truly significant breakthrough has occurred.

Chapter 18

THE LAW OF LOVE

The current of love, intimacy and intense vulnerability that runs in and through those who have gathered around me over time has attracted many, but has also repelled others. That is because I have never been able to divorce the experience of love from its absolute demand.

The extraordinary revelation of true love is over-whelming in its depth. When the floodgates have opened, it completely unhinges the lover temporarily from all points of reference—past, present or future. In that vast expanse there is only love, and in that love only perfect goodness. The power of this kind of revelation is usually like an earthquake that literally shakes to pieces all previously held assumptions about the nature of reality and the meaning of existence. In its wake is left a heart that has been opened so painfully wide that it has eclipsed all fear and has annihilated all doubt. Wounded by absolute love, the lover now knows the truth. In light of that knowledge, the lover has to answer the question: are they willing and able to live up to love's demands? *Are they willing and able to be an undivided expression of that love in a world that is characterized by fear, doubt and division?* The unconditional demand of love is to *be* it, and in order to be it we have to be willing to come out from any and all hiding places in time and in history, from all that is false, wrong and untrue. We have to be willing to stand alone—*in* that *as* that.

At the end of my own first experience of profound revelation at the age of sixteen came the following message from the unknown: "If you surrender your life to me and me alone, you will have nothing to fear." It was clear at that moment that if I chose to do otherwise, I would indeed have a lot to fear. Fifteen years later, several weeks after I had met my last teacher, I woke up early one morning and without a trace of premeditation heard myself utter the words out loud: "My life is yours, do with me what you will." I saw before me a vast whirlpool that was life itself and into which I allowed myself to be consumed. At that moment, I knew my life would no longer be my own, for it was then that I abandoned my future, and in that all hope and all fear. From that moment on, there has been nothing left to do.

True love and the absolute freedom that it brings demands everything from us. As long as we want to have anything for ourselves, even freedom itself, we will not find true emancipation in this life. True love demands everything, and liberation, which is its reward, can only be ours when we are willing to sacrifice even that.

"Thy will be done" is the war cry "I surrender!" of the true seeker who has now become a finder. Only love, only love, only love. Only that, only that, only that. Not *my* will, but *thy* will be done.

What has always intrigued me is how many people appear to be interested in the experience of love while they so often seem mysteriously able to avoid its implications. This is part of the reason why, I think, in recent years so many have been able to spend a significant amount of time in the company of powerful spiritual teachers, attracted to and absorbed in the experience of love, without that experience necessarily having a deeper impact than one of feeling better.

Many have been drawn to me initially because of the experience of love that they have felt in my presence. And while the majority may be more than satisfied with that, for me it has never been enough. I have never been able to allow those who have come to me to settle merely for the experience of feeling better. While bliss indeed may temporarily create the illusion that all is well, in most cases underneath that bliss still lies the demon of ignorance, ready to strike as soon as the bliss fades or when the ego is challenged once again.

If the experience of love and bliss is not merely a superficial event, then in that experience must be the revelation of the emptiness of a separate or personal self. That means, therefore, that ideally bliss becomes not the possession or mere object of fascination for the ego, but that ocean of being within which the ego loses its balance and all points of reference. When all points of reference have truly been lost, then there is only that and nothing else.

It is because the demand to drown and truly lose oneself in that ocean for eternity is not made often enough that so many seekers end up satisfied with being mere voyeurs of their own Self, rather than living expressions of it. Because the attachment to the ego and the world of becoming is so strong, most seekers feel deeply threatened by the possibility of drowning forever.

The course of my life as a teacher has been defined by my continuous insistence that the experience of love and bliss is meaningless when it is not supported by a life lived with true integrity. Integrity, in a life based on the pursuit of freedom, is the unconditional willingness to renounce all that has been discovered to be false, wrong and untrue. Ironically, it is because of this that I have been the object of much controversy.

In retrospect, I can see now that even from early on this was my message, implicitly if not directly. Little did I know that this would often pose what appeared to be an almost overwhelming challenge for many. The integrity, or lack of it, in the manner in which one lived one's life became an issue of fundamental importance for those who gathered around me from the very beginning. In fact, for those who became one with me in spirit, it soon was expected that integrity or pure-hearted motivation be the expression of one's response to the experience of love and bliss. It was precisely this that simultaneously attracted some and repelled others.

The call was absolute, and the response ultimately had to be also for the circle to remain unbroken. The very substance of that circle was love. In that circle there was no division and no difference. But if true love was the very substance of that circle then any and all obstacles to that love had to be given up, because true love demands the renunciation of all that is false, wrong and untrue—if one is going to be able to truly dissolve into it. Such is the law of love. It is only through allowing the law of love to become manifest *as ourselves* that the profound evolutionary leap can occur in which Love and Truth can finally become indistinguishable. This is the whole point of spiritual life.

Chapter 19

TRUTH IS STRANGER
THAN FICTION

In the summer of 1990, I returned to western Massachusetts to teach for two weeks and while there was invited to meet the world-famous yogi and teacher Amrit Desai. Several of my students and I first were given a tour of the grounds and facilities of his very impressive Kripalu Center for Yoga and Health in Lenox, and then were taken to meet him at his beautiful house near the main building. I had known about him for several years and had been impressed by what I had read about his mastery of the life force, which in yogic terminology is called prana. Several hundred people live as permanent members of his ashram while hundreds of others visit for short periods of time for different kinds of health-oriented programs and meditation and yoga courses.

A beautiful man in his early fifties, Yogi Desai has long dark hair that falls down to his shoulders and a radiant face with refined features. We spent three hours together during which he was extremely gracious and hospitable.

We spoke about many different topics, including the sub-
ject of spiritual community. Although he is a man of his
time, in many ways life for the formal residents of his
ashram is lived in a traditional Indian manner. Most men
and women practice celibacy, live separately and are even
encouraged to socialize with one another as little as possible
in order to avoid temptation and distraction. I was struck
by what seemed to be an old-fashioned and unrealistic way
to deal with the difficult question of sexuality and relationship in the spiritual life. Also, it apparently wasn't
working very well. Before I went in to see Yogi Desai, some
of his students had told me that in spite of the emphasis
on celibacy, there was still a fair amount of clandestine
sexual activity in the ashram. When I told him that many
of my own students practiced celibacy he became very
interested, but was visibly shocked when I said that some
men and women shared rooms together. Shock seemed to
turn to disbelief though when I told him that there had
never been any sexual misconduct, in spite of the fact that
there was so much intimate contact.

I remember being a little surprised by Yogi Desai's
response. But it wasn't the first time. I have seen people
respond in ways much more extreme than Yogi Desai's to
what apparently has become an almost unthinkable possibility. That the law of love could become manifest to such a
degree that people *could* find a way to truly come together
in an extraordinary manner. That an intimacy so profound

existed that it defied all cynicism and doubt—an intimacy so pure that in its presence maya could find no hiding place in which to preserve the illusion of a separate existence.

For many years now, I have been surprised to find how rare is the knowledge of true intimacy. On one hand, far too many people don't believe that it's possible; and on the other, most are deeply terrified of actually finding it. This has been and continues to be the most mind-boggling aspect of my journey through life as a spiritual teacher. Ironically, even in the modern spiritual world more seem to be threatened by the possibility of truly coming together than are really interested in it. That is because the price that needs to be paid for the experience of true intimacy to become more than a brief interlude is *real* ego death. The kind of vulnerability that that demands seems far too terrifying for anyone who is not yet interested in going all the way home in this life.

Because the law of love demands such a high price from the seeker after Truth, those who are not ready to go all the way seek for easier routes. They seek for bargains. Bargains can indeed be found, but time will reveal them to be only cheap imitations that masquerade as the real thing. As long as the seeker wants to survive, as long as the seeker still wants to be somebody *and* be free, the result can only be a condition that continues to be fundamentally divided. Indeed, the whole point of spiritual practice and experience is to finally come to the end of that division, and so as long as the seeker has not yet come to that point where they are ready to make the necessary sacrifices to become whole, the result of spiritual practice and experience will usually be more of the same. It is a constant revelation to me the way in which people who are not yet ready to make those sacrifices choose to accept and subscribe to partial and corrupt views about enlightenment, simply because they serve to shield them from the overwhelming implications of having to come to a final reckoning with life and all of their karma, absolutely and without conditions.

If we desire liberation, if we sincerely want to know what it means to be free in this life, then to win that freedom we have to be willing to unconditionally accept responsibility for our actions, past, present and future. We have to be willing to wholeheartedly come to a final reckoning with life for the first and last time. This is what it means to die unconditionally. One of the traditional definitions of enlightenment is that once enlightened, one ceases to create karma, which I define as no longer acting out of ignorance in such a way that causes suffering to others. To be fully enlightened would mean that not only is one no longer creating karma, but one has also destroyed or burned all the karma that one has ever created. That means that for the one who is fully awake, there is no longer any karmic debt to pay—nothing left undone and nothing left to do.

Each time we act out of ignorance, a momentum is generated that over time accumulates weight, speed and mass. Through constant repetition this movement becomes self-generating. Gradually, this movement, which is ignorance, becomes a tremendous and very destructive force. It is the veiling power of this karmic momentum that creates the wall of separation and isolation that is ego. It is only through the cultivation of an unshakable willingness and unwavering determination to take responsibility for every last drop of all of it, that we can even hope to attain genuine liberation in this life.

It's a mad world and truth *is* stranger than fiction. I never would have guessed that my mere insistence that it is possible to be free as long as we are willing to be held accountable for our actions could cause grown men and women to run for their lives in fear. And not only that, but could cause intelligent and even some deeply awakened people to defy the laws of common sense.

For several years now I have stated that *what we do is who we are*—not what we think and not what we feel. What we choose to do or not do is the unambiguous expression of what we have realized and how far we have come. This has caused quite a reaction. When asked, "Do you believe that a guru is responsible for his actions? Is this a valid way of determining the quality of a teacher?," questions obviously inspired by my apparently controversial teaching, my former teacher gave himself away. "First of all, the guru is not commanded by any person. He is a free man. No one can command him. Not even God can command him. God listens to his commands," he said. So upset was he by my absolute stand that he went so far as to tell his chief disciple to literally follow me to the four corners of the world in order to "purify the corruption" I was spreading.

"Andrew the righteous one," the Indian professor of physics said to me in a barely veiled, mocking tone as we were having breakfast together at a yoga and consciousness research conference in Bangalore, India. I had just finished reading "A Crisis of Trust" from this book to the audience at the conference. It was the professor himself who had arranged for me to speak there. "You're setting yourself up for a fall," he said. At first I was dumbfounded, surprised at the intensity of the feeling with which he was speaking to me. We had met six months earlier and I had been particularly impressed with him. When speaking together about spiritual matters, to my delight, because of his scientific background he was able to be objective in a way that most spiritual practitioners, including many teachers, seem to have a lot of trouble with. I was stunned to see him now expressing the same outrage I had experienced from others at my insistence that if enlightenment was to mean something truly significant, then a high ethical standard had to be upheld.

Ever amazed and even sometimes amused to discover that my emphasis on integrity is interpreted as a form of spiritual fascism by many, I often wonder if I have lost my mind.

When some of my students were speaking to a well-known Buddhist journalist about writing an article, he responded with disinterest, saying he didn't want to have anything to do with the controversy surrounding my breakup with my teacher. Then his face brightened and he said, "But if there were a scandal around Andrew, now that would make a very interesting article."

(Truth is indeed stranger than fiction....

I had always respected Yogi Desai for the fact that in a time when almost all the great Indian yogis who had come to the West to spread the ancient teachings had fallen in disgrace, he stood alone as an example of purity and integrity. Four years after I met him, during the editing of this book, the Yogi's shock and disbelief at the fact that male and female students of mine could share rooms together without incidents of sexual misconduct was explained. A widely publicized scandal broke revealing that the Yogi, a married man who had stressed celibacy for his own students, had been carrying on affairs with his female students for over ten years.)

THE SCIENCE
OF ENLIGHTENMENT

Chapter 20

THE PROBLEM WITH ADVAITA

"You're just like the oil fields in Kuwait," he said to me emphatically, shaking his head.

Confused, I turned to my student who was sitting next to me and asked, "Do you understand what he's getting at?"

"No," he said to me equally confused.

I was sitting outside the American Hotel in Amsterdam, having coffee with a well-known Dutch teacher of Advaita Vedanta, a disciple of the highly respected master of Advaita, Nisargadatta Maharaj. As I had been teaching there almost every summer, over the years we had heard quite a bit about each other. It was he who had initiated our meeting. As we spoke, the feeling between us was undoubtedly warm, permeated by an unmistakable intensity as we were in the midst of trying to figure each other out.

"You're just like the oil fields in Kuwait," he repeated.

"What do you mean?" I asked.

"After eight years of teaching you're still burning, you're still on fire!"

"Yes," I replied.

"But what you're trying to do won't work. You'll be disillusioned."

"You're cynical!" I said.

"Of course I am," he responded without hesitation. "I've been teaching for fifteen years and nobody's changed, nobody!"

I had met several of his students and he was right. In spite of the fact that many of them had indeed, with his help, experienced glimpses of nonduality, that fundamental shift that brings with it a profound trust in life had not occurred. He was undoubtedly an awakened man, and from all the reports I had heard, a powerful teacher.

He seemed to be simultaneously intrigued and shocked at the stand I was taking. The fact that I had spoken out about the inconsistent and often outrageous behavior of some modern spiritual teachers (including him) amazed him.

With genuine sincerity and even a trace of innocence, he asked, "But how can you judge? How can anyone judge?"

From his perspective, the nondual teachings of Advaita philosophy, there is only THAT. There is no doer and there is no other. Beyond the mind with all its ideas, thoughts and conclusions, beyond shoulds and shouldn'ts, everything simply IS. From that perspective, drawing conclusions about anything can be seen as an expression of ignorance. Beyond good and evil, beyond cause and effect, beyond birth and death, there is only THAT.

"You and I and everyone here judge," I said as I waved my hand pointing toward the people seated at the tables nearby, and then to others walking across the square in front of us. "In our hearts we all know what the truth is."

Shaking his head incredulously, he said, "I have compassion for you. You're going to be crucified."

"I don't need your compassion. I need your support," I responded.

"You have it," he said to my surprise.

Later I asked the Dutch teacher about his meeting with his guru, whom I had heard so much about but had never had the privilege to meet.

"The first time we met, I told him that I knew a lot. I told him that intellectually maybe I knew more than he did. But then I said that in my heart I knew I didn't know anything and I asked for his help."

He went on to describe to me how within a short time spent in the company of this extraordinary teacher, all of his questions were answered. This resulted in an explosion of awakening which brought his seeking to a sudden and final end. "After that," he said, "there was nothing left for me to do." Nisargadatta Maharaj soon asked him to teach others and then encouraged him to stay on for a while so that he could observe what was happening there, saying it would be of help to him in the future.

"I have only one desire left," he said. "I wish I could

have the opportunity to sit and drink tea with him one more time. Just to sit and drink tea together. That's all."

After a while I said something that apparently surprised the Dutch teacher: "I don't feel that Advaita is a comprehensive enough teaching to meet the genuine needs of most seekers."

His instant reply was, "You obviously don't know what you're talking about."

"Wait," I said. "There is no doubt it is a perfect teaching, a perfect jewel. But it is a teaching that can only work perfectly for someone who is already very pure, for someone in whom the veil of delusion is very, very thin. Also, most seekers need a teaching that will embrace every aspect of the human condition," I went on to say. "The nondual teachings don't do that."

"You've got so many assumptions!" the Dutch teacher said in a way that left me no doubt that he thought I was *very* misinformed.

For several years I had thought a lot about this. Indeed, my own teacher had been a disciple of Ramana Maharshi, and so I was not unfamiliar with his message or his nondual teaching. As a matter of fact, the shocking experiential revelation that *only the Self exists,* along with my teacher's emphasis on letting go of all effort and striving, had catapulted me beyond the chains of memory, fear and doubt. When I started to teach, this same message had been my message also. It was after a few years of teaching though that I began to slowly reconsider these fundamental ideas as their efficacy had been brought into question by two events that began to occur in my life simultaneously. On one side, it became obvious that the complexity of the human condition demanded a teaching that was far more comprehensive in its approach than one that was based upon the ceaseless stressing of the unreality of anything other than a single, absolute principle. And on the other side, the fact that the glaring inconsistencies and outrageous hypocrisy in the conduct of my own teacher could be so easily justified by him and those around him with the very same nondual teaching that he was using to set people free forced me to stand back and reconsider everything once again.

Ceaseless insistence that the Self is the only reality indeed can have a powerful effect. That effect, of course, being the explosive insight into the ultimately undivided condition of reality Absolute. The shock that this kind of revelation has on the system can awaken a person in a dramatic way. But because most individuals are usually not yet prepared for the depth of surrender necessary that allows that kind of experience to be the catalyst for true liberation from fear, ignorance and delusion, its result is usually short-lived and its ultimate significance is often overexaggerated.

Most seekers, I had found, needed a teaching that not only stressed the inherent oneness of life, but one that would also simultaneously encourage them to look directly into the intricate relationship between thought and feeling. Insight that revealed the delicate interplay of the cause and effect that occurs between the subtle dimension of mind and the seemingly grosser manifestation of the outer world needed to be cultivated in most through continuous contemplation and meditation. Precisely because the mind's ability to endlessly create and recreate false notions of self is so staggering in its subtlety, this subtlety *must* be discovered again and again until the individual not only experiences temporary insight, but actually *remains* awake. Time and experience showed me over and over again that for most, mere insistence that the Self is the only reality was not sufficient to reveal the depth and subtlety of the nature of mind and its movement to the degree necessary to win deep and lasting liberation from confusion and delusion.

Also I had seen and met far too many people over the years I had been teaching, students and teachers alike, who misused the nondual teaching as a way to avoid or deny aspects of themselves. This, surprisingly enough, was often done in the name of liberation itself. The nondual teaching inadvertently leaves loopholes that all too easily allow an imperfect attainment to masquerade as one that is perfect and complete. My Dutch peer was a good example of this. When asked by one of his students if his womanizing in any way pointed to the fact that maybe he wasn't free, his response was, "No. These are just my tendencies burning themselves out." In many ways he reminded me of my own teacher, insofar as the way he lived his life seemed to be such an extreme contradiction of the absolute nature of his own teaching.

The fundamental tenet of the nondual teaching is that we are always already free. From that point of view, one whose motives are not yet entirely pure and yet who has attained a significant degree of awakening can easily justify almost any expression of ignorance with outrageous statements like "there is *no doer*" and "all is unreal—only the *Self* exists!"

Indeed, if one is already free, from the point of view of the nondual teaching there is nowhere to go, nothing to do and *definitely* nothing to change because everything simply IS. All too often, this absolute fact is used as a justification for allowing oneself to remain ignorant, rather than as a genuine vehicle for true emancipation.

"I admit I've made some mistakes," my Dutch peer said. "I'm not perfect. *Nobody's* perfect. Anyway, don't believe everything that you hear. As a matter of fact, I've heard that *you* are a homosexual!"

My Dutch friend often punctuated his remarks by whacking me powerfully on the shoulder. In spite of the fact that there was obvious disagreement between us, the atmosphere remained lighthearted until the end. As we parted, we gave each other a big hug.

I, along with countless others, marvel at the unparalleled manifestation of perfect purity, love and utter selflessness that the great Ramana Maharshi was and continues to represent. It has often occurred to me that the reason he has become so well known throughout the world over the last twenty years may be more because he has become a symbol of purity, proof of what is possible for all of us, than because of his teaching of self-inquiry—the passionate pursuit of the question "Who am I?" Indeed, in a world that has become so deeply cynical and overburdened with misery, one such as he stands out like the North Star on a clear night. Like a beacon of hope, the fact that he walked this earth so recently is living proof to all whose hearts have grown weary that perfect goodness *does* exist. The example of his life, a perfect expression of undivided, absolute simplicity and pure motivation without a trace of selfishness, is what challenges even the most jaded observer to look into their own heart. What is important to acknowledge, I feel, is that it was his utter authenticity as a *human being* that allowed him to make the most outrageously absolute statements about life and death, love and truth, without one feeling in any way compelled to doubt their legitimacy.

One who speaks only of that which is undivided, single and absolute must be an expression of that which is undivided, single and absolute for their words to carry the weight of genuine authority. From all I have heard from those who had the good fortune to spend time in his company, Nisargadatta Maharaj was also such a one. Indeed, a life without fundamental contradiction that speaks of love and unity dares us to become whole ourselves. A life expressing fundamental contradiction, yet that speaks of love and unity, does not and cannot truly challenge our hearts in such a way that would force us to rise up to meet it without conditions.

Chapter 21

HEAVEN, EARTH AND CREATION

Three weeks after I had met my last teacher, we were sitting quietly together in a park in Lucknow in northern India. I was pondering over my newfound realization that everything simply IS. "There's nothing to do and nowhere to go," I said, breaking the silence. "After awakening one sees clearly that nothing needs to change because everything is perfect as it is."

"Very good," he responded.

A few moments later I asked him, "Why then did the Buddha start a sangha? Why did he encourage people to give up the world and follow him in order to lead a life of renunciation together, outside of and apart from the secular world?"

"I don't know," he said, shaking his head.

At the time, this seemed to be a contradiction to the realization of the inherent perfection of things as they are. The desire to move away from, to change in any way, seemed to be the very antithesis of that radical understanding.

Why, I wanted to know, did Ramana Maharshi, my teacher's teacher, discourage his disciples from making any external changes in their lives in order to facilitate their awakening, while the Buddha encouraged so many to give up all for the sake of enlightenment? There was no question that these two men stood as peerless examples of the highest spiritual attainment. It was not irrelevant, therefore, that their teachings differed so significantly.

It wasn't until five years had passed that I finally began to understand the answer to that question. During the first retreat that I taught in Bodhgaya in 1991, I took long walks with some of my closest students in the dusty fields just beyond the main temple. As we walked and talked, a massive stone statue of the Buddha sitting serenely in a meditation posture stared at us from the edge of town. It was then that I began to inquire in a way that I never had before.

It occurred to me that enlightenment was not necessarily all one and the same. It began to dawn on me that although the absolute nature of enlightenment must be one and the same, the different expressions of enlightenment in apparently fully awakened individuals could be based on conclusions about its significance that were not necessarily the same.

For the first few years of my teaching career, my spontaneous response to those who came to me was: realize and surrender. Realize that mystery that cannot be understood by the mind. Upon the discovery of that mystery, surrender to that and that alone. Realize and surrender. Realize and surrender. Realize and surrender.

Realize that you were never born. Surrender to the fact that you were never unfree. Realize there was never a problem and never back down from that realization. Surrender to that and that alone.

What more could there be to it? What more could there be? Nothing. Nothing. Nothing.

Spontaneously this message, this transmission of love and joy streamed through me, touching the hearts of those who dared to believe even for an instant that it could be so simple.

The fact that heaven was at hand, that it had never been distant but was always nearer than near, ready to be found like a long lost love, was a constant revelation to me and to those who gathered around me.

In heaven there is nothing to do and nowhere to go. Or is there?

With time and experience the same current coming from that mystery began to carry a different cadence. The message began to change. Why? Because it became more and more apparent that heaven was *not* separate from earth.

In heaven there was no doer. In heaven there was no other, there was no cause and there was no effect. On earth there was a doer, there was another, there was cause and effect.

Herein lay the greatest challenge for any genuine teaching of enlightenment. To reveal that perfect middle place between all pairs of opposites—that most profound point where heaven and earth meet and become indistinguishable. This seemed to be not only the greatest challenge for any teaching of enlightenment, but also the greatest challenge for the seeker after enlightenment. The extraordinary subtlety in this seemed so easy to miss. For even though the deepest spiritual insight was the revelation of that perfect middle place where heaven and earth meet, few seemed to be able to sustain that depth of transparency for more than a brief instant. Indeed, what often posed as the pursuit of enlightenment, closer scrutiny revealed to be none other than a path of *escape* from earth. In that escape the fundamental foundation of ignorance—which is a dualistic relationship to life—not only was not destroyed, but unknowingly became even more pronounced.

This was why the message began to change. This was why the fact that heaven was not separate from earth now became my constant refrain.

What then began to unfold was extraordinary. The current coming from that mystery now began to uncover a view in which earth didn't have to disappear in order to realize heaven. More importantly, realizing heaven was not enough—for now *to literally manifest heaven on earth* became an unavoidable and irreconcilable necessity if awakening was to be truly profound. This movement—

bringing the living fact of heaven, of unity, into time and space, into being—revealed itself to be an *evolutionary imperative*. The call to *be* that which is undivided overtook the significance of the mere discovery of that which is undivided.

The thrill was uncontainable as the evolutionary impulse that expressed itself as boundless energy wanted only that that perfect love and unity become manifest in time and space. As what? As perfect relationship between self and other, self and world. The meaning of nonduality seemed to take on even greater significance. Heaven was not separate from earth—but that fact now had to be proven through the unconditional willingness to become the living expression of that which is undivided as self.

The movement of the big bang, of creation itself, was revealed in all its glory. Miraculously the very structures that contain and sustain ignorance and impede evolution were seen through while simultaneously structures that contain and sustain love and unity came into being. So much became possible and so much passion to realize that possibility expressed itself. Indeed, there seemed to be *so much* to do!

In the response to the call to be that which is undivided, there was no way to escape from earth. In fact, the call to be that which is undivided demanded that all impulses to remain divided, which means separate, be transcended. It became obvious that only through perfect renunciation and transcendence of the impulse to remain separate, would the individual be able to manifest that transparency which was the very expression of the point where heaven and earth meet and become indistinguishable.

Walking back toward the main temple, it was clear in a way that it never had been before the degree to which my own perspective had changed. It seemed that Ramana Maharshi and the Buddha actually were speaking about different expressions of enlightenment. While there was no doubt in my mind that both of these extraordinary men were full-blown manifestations of the miracle of profound spiritual awakening—the discovery of and perfect abidance in that perfect middle place between all pairs of opposites— the expression of those realizations pointed to the fact that they had come to conclusions that were not necessarily the same. The former seemed to be pointing to the discovery of and permanent abidance in heaven. The latter, the necessity of bringing heaven to earth. It became apparent now why one discouraged his disciples from making any external changes in their lives in order to awaken, while the other, for the same reason, encouraged so many to give up everything and come together.

Three years later, I went to visit a Kabbalistic scholar who lived with his family in a small village of Hasidic Jews in the desert just outside Tel Aviv.

"The basic principle of the mystical way of Judaism is called 'ratzo vashov'," he said. "Ratzo vashov means a continual, living dynamic of the terms of run and return. Run and return means running out of confinement and being able to return into that previous state of confinement in order to rectify it....In some way God created the world in order for us to bring his infinite light into this finite existence. That's the purpose, that's utopia."

Chapter 22

MOTHER OF THE UNIVERSE

In the summer of 1994, I was invited to teach in southern France. The occasion was unusual. I was invited there by another spiritual teacher to speak to a large gathering of mostly his own students. We had met for the first time several years earlier in Israel and had become friends. During this, my second visit, my wife and I stayed as houseguests with him, his wife and their two teenage children. They were gracious hosts and our meals together were always festive gatherings, with friends, other teachers, writers and students in attendance. These times were often highlighted by serious and occasionally intense dialogue.

It was during those meals together that I met a German man and his wife, who had been specifically invited by my host to spend some time informally with me. My host had told me that this man had been a longtime devotee of one of the most famous Indian female gurus of our time. He said that his friend had recently left her and was still very upset and confused about what had happened. Knowing my own story, my host thought that I might be able to help him.

His guru was known for her extraordinary compassion and unconditional love. I had read about her and had been very impressed by her purity, utter abandon and intense ecstasy. Affectionately called "Mother" by her devotees, she was supposed to be an Avatar (an incarnation of God, the rarest and highest manifestation of enlightenment) and thousands flocked to receive her blessings as she traveled around the world.

During the weekend, over lunches and dinners together, he told me his story. He said that he had met his guru fifteen years earlier, well before she had become famous. He had lived in her intimate company for the first few years and had taken a formal vow of brahmacharya (celibacy). Along with long hours of meditation, he spent the rest of his time in her service. His descriptions of her were both marvelous and intriguing. There was no doubt that she was a profoundly awakened human being whose experience of the Absolute was far beyond the bounds of most. He said that after nine years with her in India, she asked him to go to Europe and serve her teaching work there. This involved setting up and procuring ashrams, arranging her travel schedule and representing her through teaching in her name. She said that when necessary she would "speak through" him. Surviving on what were only meager donations, he described to me how he worked for her tirelessly, eighteen hours a day every single day. He said that because of this, at one point he became so sick that he almost died.

After fifteen years in her service, he asked her permission to give up his vow of brahmacharya. He told her that for some time he felt he had been living a lie. She responded by saying that she didn't care he was living a lie, and went on to say that if he gave up his vow it would weaken the resolve of the other brahmacharyas. He described how in her way of thinking, giving up celibacy was tantamount to giving up true spiritual life altogether. After some time, he felt he had to be true to himself in spite of her refusal to meet his request and took the bold step of marrying one of her western devotees. According to his story, they were both summarily rejected from her circle and denounced as having gone back to the "world." This was apparently unbearably painful for both of them as she was not only the center of their universe, but to them was literally none other than God incarnate. The agony of this separation from their beloved was written in the lines in their faces. His wife, to my surprise, even expressed a fear that their guru had put a "curse" on them. Seeing the terror in her eyes, I couldn't help but encourage her to begin to make the effort to question some of her ideas and also to be willing to take greater responsibility for the choice that she had made. This was to no avail.

Then the story became even more complex. He described how over his years as her servant in Europe, he had accepted large donations in her name and at her request had funneled them all through his personal bank account, apparently because she felt the governments in the West were as corrupt as in India. He said now, years later, he was living in fear of the day that the government would ask him to pay taxes on that money. He was afraid he would have to go to jail. He said that he was at that time in negotiation with her lawyers, asking only that they provide him with a written statement saying that none of the money had been his own, but had all been given to her. So far they had been unwilling to do so.

Over breakfast on Sunday morning, to my surprise my host told me an alarming story about yet another world-renowned incarnation of the divine mother, Mother Meera, who is also considered to be an Avatar. The story is by now well known. Her longtime devotee and messenger, the famous scholar and poet Andrew Harvey had left her. Harvey, openly homosexual, claimed that his former guru was homophobic. He said that she wanted to break up his relationship with his male lover and told him that he had the choice of either being celibate or getting married to a woman. If he chose to marry, she wanted him to write a book about how the force of the divine mother trans-formed him into a heterosexual. He even claimed that she censored some of his writings, removing all references to his homosexuality.

I took a deep breath and turned my head, momentarily taking in the stunning beauty of the rolling hills, covered here and there with thick vineyards and patches of trees that made up the landscape of this part of southern France. I thought to myself how several of my students had been to visit Mother Meera and were impressed by her purity, simplicity and love.

I was amazed but my amazement soon turned to fascination. Both of these women were said to be Avatars, incarnations of the divine mother and living expressions of unconditional love and compassion. They were known for the depth and power of their samadhi—absorption in joy so deep and profound it was beyond description. If their love was truly unconditional, what kind of conclusions was one to draw from this? If these stories were true, what did they say about enlightenment?

What I found so fascinating was that these two remarkable women, in spite of their rare, extraordinary and unquestioned spiritual attainment, still seemed to be attached to fixed ideas! The knowledge of and ability to express a love that was profound beyond measure, the experience of and ability to share intoxicating bliss and joy apparently were not necessarily enough to liberate the mind. This was staggering.

For some time it had been clear to me that one definition of enlightenment is none other than the attainment of freedom from all fixed ideas. Why? *Because it is the liberating experience of freedom from all fixed ideas which alone enables the awakened individual to see clearly.* Indeed, it is precisely because of the freedom from all fixed ideas that the awakened individual is able to discriminate in a way that is profound, extraordinary and evolutionary.

Without that attainment, even unquestioned purity is not enough to insure that the powerful and penetrating discrimination that is the expression of a truly liberated mind will arise. Without it, that perfect response that is the consistent manifestation of the attainment of that middle place between all pairs of opposites where heaven and earth meet will not occur.

Chapter 23

THE SCIENCE OF ENLIGHTENMENT

Imagine a mirror. Imagine that the surface of that mirror is completely covered with dried mud, with not even a trace of the surface of that mirror visible. This is the state of unqualified ignorance.

Now imagine that for some mysterious reason the surface of this mirror is suddenly struck by a bolt of lightning. The tremendous force of the impact removes a small portion of the dried mud from the surface, exposing it to the light of day. Instantly the small portion of the surface of the mirror that has been exposed begins to reflect the light of the sun that is shining down upon it.

This is the birth of awakening. This is the birth of enlightenment.

Such an individual stands out. For now in the middle of their shadow is a small hole. The light of the Self that shines through them stands in obvious, stark contrast to the ignorance that is the expression of most of those who surround them.

Now imagine another. Imagine that the force of the lightning that has struck the surface of the mirror of this one is five times as powerful as the first. The impact was such that now literally half the entire surface of the mirror has been exposed to the light of day.

This one casts a reflection that is very bright. This one also stands in stark contrast to the other, literally outshining them with their brilliance.

This one casts only half a shadow. This one is rare.

Now imagine yet another. Imagine that the force of the lightning that has struck the surface of this one is so overpowering that the sheer weight of its impact has removed ninety percent of the mud that covered it, exposing ninetenths of the surface of the mirror to the light of day. The reflection of the sun is now overwhelming.

The shadow cast by this one is a small dot that is barely visible to the naked eye. This one is magnificent, extraordinary and almost beyond compare, because this one leaves almost no trace.

Finally imagine one last one. Imagine in this case that the force of the lightning that has struck the surface of the mirror has been so explosive that it has removed all of the mud that once covered it. In this case there is not even one speck of dust left on the surface of the mirror.

This one casts no shadow. This one casts only a perfect reflection. This one leaves no trace.

THE UNKNOWN
CAN ONLY
BE UNKNOWN

Chapter 24

THE UNKNOWN
CAN ONLY BE UNKNOWN

On a warm September evening in 1994, my wife and I were standing on the corner of 53rd Street and Park Avenue in New York City waiting for the light to change. We were on our way to the Theosophical Society where I was going to be giving a talk and were both looking forward to the evening ahead. The audiences who came to see me in New York were almost always enthusiastic and unselfconscious in their response to my teaching.

When the light changed, we stepped off the curb. The row of taxicabs that made up the front line of cars coming toward us all came to a halt. Then out of the corner of my eye, I saw that the car on the inside lane, also a taxi, was speeding directly at us. In that instant, I knew that it wasn't going to stop. I knew it was going to hit us. Then it happened. With a loud bang, the cab hit the right side of my body. Then I heard the sound of impact again as it crashed into two cars that were crossing the intersection. My arm dropped and began dangling and I became aware of a dull pressure in my right leg. My body going into shock, I felt like I had been injected with a powerful drug. Numb and dazed, I was at the same time very alert. Looking down I saw my wife lying on her back, eyes half closed, with blood streaming out of her mouth. Then I heard voices screaming at me from the curb, "Lie down, lie down." I lowered myself to the ground as people wanting to help surrounded me. Short of breath and finding it difficult to speak, I asked them to call an ambulance. While waiting, I lifted up my head several times to look over at my wife, only to find that she was not moving. This was always met by fierce objections from the concerned strangers gathered around. Later I was told that within minutes, 53rd Street and Park Avenue looked like a war zone. The entire area was immediately cordoned off, with broken glass all over the street, police everywhere, TV cameras, flashing lights and crowds of people trying to see what happened.

Like angels descending from heaven, an emergency medical team suddenly appeared and put an oxygen mask over my nose and mouth. "How ya doin' pal?" one of the angels asked. "Do you know what day this is? Do you know where you are?" "Yes," I responded.

Feeling strangely peaceful, it occurred to me how great it would be if this were all only a dream. Unfortunately, I knew it wasn't.

For most of the ambulance ride to the hospital, I

thought to myself how utterly stupid, how utterly pointless this whole event was.

Soon after I arrived in the emergency room, it was determined that I was a lucky man. For even though my right arm had been badly broken and my right calf had been ripped open so severely the bone was completely exposed, there were no internal or spinal injuries. Briefly pausing to look directly into the face of death, I experienced shock and dismay at the thought that my life could have come to an end when it seemed like my work was only beginning. At the same time, I knew beyond any doubt in a way that is difficult to describe in words that it wasn't my time yet.

"Your wife's going to be OK," one of the doctors told me after a half hour had passed. "She suffered a bad concussion and has a fracture in her upper jaw. But she's had a CAT scan and her brain hasn't been injured." I was relieved.

After my arm had been set in a temporary cast, my leg was sewn up by an intern who told me not to look until he was finished. This took well over two hours. During this time, a few of my students were allowed to come in and sit with me.

"The cab went straight through a red light, hit both of you and then ran into two cars going west on 53rd Street," one of my students said as the intern worked intently on my leg.

"What happened to the cab driver?" I asked.

"I saw the police pulling him out through the window

of his cab completely covered in blood," he responded. "I don't know what happened after that."

"Those goddamn taxis!" a surgeon exclaimed, over-hearing our conversation. "Eighty percent of our trauma cases are from accidents involving taxis," he said irately.

"Really?" I replied, expressing shock and disbelief.

"There's an epidemic," he went on to say. "Last night a man came in who had been hit by a cab going seventy miles an hour down a side street. When he came in, his face was this big," he said, holding his hands about two feet away from each other. "He had no face left. Tomorrow morning we're going to do a sixteen-hour operation to try and put his face back together."

Why had this happened? What did it all mean? On and off throughout the entire ordeal that had unexpectedly begun to unfold that evening I asked myself these questions. I tried to find some kind of meaning in it. I was seeking for a clue that would unlock the mystery of how and why something like this had occurred. The only meaning that I could possibly find was that I should slow down. But almost as soon as this conclusion popped into my head, the absurdity of it became apparent. Slow down? For whom? For what? And why? It made no sense. I was a young man who had so much energy. To do what? To do *exactly* what it was that I had been doing. The passion that welled up from inside me wouldn't permit me to lead any other life than the one I had been leading.

The utter senselessness of it all, the random and indiscriminate nature of chaos that is a fundamental fact of life, was there staring me right in the face—naked and unrepentant. There is a part of human nature that seeks to justify each and every event that occurs, that always strains to find meaning even where there may not necessarily be any. In what I was facing into there was no satisfaction to be found. There was only a big question mark.

I thought about how lucky my wife and I had been. One more inch and most likely one or both of us would have been dead or crippled beyond repair. I thought about the poor man who now, as the surgeon described to me, was lying upstairs in the hospital with a maze of tubes going into his throat, his face so disfigured that it was just a mass of flesh and bone. What did *that* mean? He had been hit, as I had, by a cab that was speeding and out of control.

It takes courage to accept and come to terms with that which seems unjust and yet does not inherently contain any personal meaning or significance. In both cases, no doubt the cab drivers were at fault, but in a crazy and unfair world they had their own reasons for being out of control at that moment. Many of the taxi drivers in New York are new immigrants, a significant number of whom can hardly speak English. I was told shortly after the accident that the drivers live under a tremendous amount of pressure. They have to pay an extremely high daily fee to rent the cabs and therefore will drive as fast as they can in order to insure the chance of making a decent profit. I was shocked to hear that some, after working long hours, come away with only thirty-five dollars in their pocket.

I thought to myself about how spiritually minded people had a particularly strong need to find personal meaning and to give significance to almost everything that happened to them. My mind wandered back to an extraordinary evening that occurred two years earlier in Boulder, Colorado, the new-age/spiritual mecca nestled safely in the foothills of the Rocky Mountains. I was giving a talk about the role that superstition plays in the minds of far too many seekers. I described to the audience how I had noticed that most modern-day practitioners of eastern spiritual disciplines often unwittingly appropriated the superstitious beliefs of those traditions, along with the teaching or practice that had attracted them in the first place. Then I spoke about the necessity of becoming free from superstition altogether if one wanted to be truly liberated from fear and ignorance. And I explained how superstitious beliefs were one of the props that the ego used to protect itself against the overwhelming insecurity that one had to face when looking into the unfathomable mystery of life and death.

Then something strange happened. I suddenly felt a tension that was so thick it could be cut with a knife. I looked out across the room, taking in with one glance the two hundred or so faces that were staring at me. It was unmistakable. A wall of fear had risen up from the floor to the ceiling that was astounding in its intensity. It was visceral. All I could feel was: *NO!*

I was stunned. The audience was largely made up of people who, compared to most, would be considered unusually free in their thinking, adventurous and especially open-minded. "What is it?" I thought. It was the stench of religion and superstition masquerading as informed, sophisticated, modern spiritual thinking. *It was fear of the unknown!* It was fear of not knowing—that means not being sure of what's out there, not being sure of what's in here and not being sure how it all works.

Without the willingness to become deeply unsure about all these things, no room to actually find out can reveal itself. Indeed, I found it was seldom that a human being could sustain a condition of rare vulnerability and profound interest in what was true, while simultaneously remaining free from fixed ideas, superstitious beliefs and some form of religious fundamentalism....

That reminded me of an equally fascinating moment in Tel Aviv in 1992. Just after I had finished teaching one stormy December evening, I was informed that three orthodox Hasidic gentlemen, two of whom were young rabbis, wanted to speak with me. One of my students ushered them in, and after they all sat down in a row across from me he sat in a chair facing them. I remember at that moment the odd sensation of becoming aware of the fact that he wasn't Jewish. This part of my heritage, I rarely thought about. Both of my parents had been atheists and therefore I received no Jewish education whatsoever. I was not even bar mitzvahed, I could not speak Hebrew and my knowledge of Jewish history and tradition was less than minimal. I informed my Jewish brothers of this fact but they were not perturbed. I was intrigued by the unique nature of the situation and was curious to see how it would unfold.

Our meeting was continuously punctuated by bursts of lightning and the crackling sound of thunder outside, at which times one of my Jewish brothers would immediately put his hands together, close his eyes and say a prayer out loud. They explained to me that thunder and lightning were reminders of the first cause, the explosion of creation. The prayer was an acknowledgment of that fact.

At first they asked me about my history. They wanted to know what had happened to me and how I had come to be a spiritual teacher. After I responded to this question as simply and as quickly as I was able to, they made their mission clear and unequivocal. What I was doing was nice, but I was Jewish. This was a fact that I had to be willing to face and come to terms with. Because I was Jewish, they explained to me, Judaism suited me more than any other path possibly could. It was in my blood, it was in my genes, it was who I was. Then they went on to make clear to me in many different ways how and why Judaism as a religious path was the highest, superior to Islam, Christianity, Hinduism and Buddhism. One of the rabbis even told me how he had originally been a Christian priest and how fortunate he was to have come to Judaism.

These were very learned and intelligent men and their arguments were intriguing. I was fascinated by their use of logic. But at the same time, I was disappointed by what seemed to be obvious rigidity and unabashed fundamentalism. This tended to make our conversation together one-sided. Doing my best to remain open-minded, I dared myself to consider the possibility that maybe they were right. As thunder and lightning continued to crackle and explode outside, I was waiting for a bolt of lightning to hit me between the eyes, the force of my Jewish heritage bringing me to my knees. I remember at that moment thinking, "What if it were all leading to this?" Half smiling to myself, I imagined what my students in Europe and America would think....But nothing happened.

"This may be your last chance," one of my Jewish brothers said to me with growing intensity. "Once you get on that plane tomorrow you don't know what will happen—you may never have this chance again!"

Their insistence soon became annoying and I was amazed to see how such obvious passion and intelligence could coexist with such fanaticism. There was no room to meet. There was no room for the unknown....

Then I remembered how during a recent trip to London, a couple who were very taken with my teaching revealed it all to me once again. For twelve years they had been disciples of the late Swami Muktananda, and like others who had been with him, had many powerful spiritual experiences. Eventually becoming disillusioned with their path and the integrity of their teacher, they left. Several months later they came to see me, which was also a powerful experience for them. Hearing me speak incessantly about the need to question all of our ideas about the nature of reality if we wanted to be free thrilled them. After so many years of being told who and what God was, they finally discovered the freedom to find out for themselves. Suddenly night seemed to turn to day and all became possible once again, as simultaneously things began to make sense that hadn't made sense before and new questions arose that pointed in the direction of yet uncharted waters. It was my emphasis on inquiry and insistence on integrity that moved them so deeply. Beaming like lightbulbs, their excitement was obvious.

But after two weeks had passed, I noticed that one of the lightbulbs began to grow dim. Then they asked to see me privately. What unfolded was extraordinary. The woman, it seemed, was going through a crisis of faith. Suddenly the very thing that had excited her the most when she had met me—radical questioning—began to terrify her. That which had been recognized as the door to liberation was now in the midst of her crisis seen as the door to hell itself.

"Before I encountered your teaching," she said, "I knew where everything was. Everything made sense. Now I don't know what's true any longer." I was amazed. In spite of all the spiritual experiences she had, without the support of a preconceived, metaphysical model to tell her who she was, where she was and what it all meant, spiritually she was lost. She was like a small boat drifting listlessly on a vast ocean without an anchor.

"Wait a minute," I said. "That's what excited you so much about this teaching in the first place. You recognized how after all this time, without realizing it, you were holding up the universe and everything in it with your mind— even all the ideas you had about God, you suddenly began to question. That's what thrilled you, that's what excited you—seeing and going beyond, finding out for yourself what's true!"

"Yes," she said. "But I no longer feel excited about it. I just feel terrified and confused."

Then it all became clear. "*You're no longer sure if God exists!* That's what the problem is, isn't it?"

"That's right," she said.

"But even if God *doesn't* exist," I said, "wouldn't you want to know the truth?"

That prospect didn't seem to excite her....

It was now 5:45 in the morning and I was lying quietly in my hospital bed staring at the ceiling. A close student of mine who had been with me for the entire night had just fallen asleep in a chair next to my bed, his head leaning gently against the wall. Aside from a dull ache in my right arm, I wasn't experiencing much pain. In the short time since the deep gash in my calf had been sewn up, the wound had become an object of fascination for me. In an odd way we had become friends.

As I lay there, I began to wonder what kind of conclusions others would draw about the meaning and significance of what had happened the night before. Then I smiled to myself, thinking about the likelihood that the conclusions my friends and supporters would draw would differ greatly from those of my detractors.

Within twenty-four hours, I was informed that my students in America and Europe had been deeply affected by the accident. The results were twofold: first, their superstitious ideas were shaken to the core, as many admitted that they never thought that something like this could happen to me. But even more importantly, they discovered a renewed sense of urgency in their own relationship to becoming free in this birth. They knew in a way they never had before that they could take nothing for granted. The preciousness of life, the immediacy of death and the unbearably delicate possibility of enlightenment were revealed in a way that was ruthless, overwhelming and profound.

Chapter 25

Is It Possible?

"Go ahead with your teachings," Penor Rinpoche said to me during a meeting we had in Bodhgaya at the beginning of 1994. "Try your best to give this to people, to make them realize that naturalness. Because after that naturalness there must be some inner space, there must arise infinite compassion to help others. That is very important. In Buddhism we say brightness itself is the essence of compassion, and compassion itself is the essence of brightness. So they must go together. But first you must realize that brightness, and arising with it there must be a lot of natural compassion."

"I am always emphasizing that the motivation for enlightenment must change from the personal to the impersonal," I responded. "I emphasize that because so many people are only concerned with their own liberation. I call this teaching Impersonal Enlightenment."

"The root of bondage, the root of suffering itself is our clinging to a nonexisting personal," Penor Rinpoche said.

"Thinking that everything is personal, though everything is always impersonal."

"Yes, this is what I mean," I replied, wholeheartedly agreeing with him.

"But we cling to everything as personal, and that is the root cause of our own bondage."

"This is the essence of my teaching," I went on to say. "The essence. I am always stressing to people to realize that there is nothing personal about anything that any human being could ever experience at any moment in time."

"A very judicious person can always know this," the Rinpoche said. "So if you get that, if you reach that impersonal level, if you can ultimately give away that clinging to the personal, that itself is actually liberation."

It was always thrilling to meet other teachers and even more so when we really met. Penor Rinpoche is head of the Nyingma lineage and also a highly respected master of Dzogchen. This meeting occurred while I was leading a two-week intensive retreat, which over the last four years had become an annual event. Once again, a large group of people had gathered together from all over the world in this small town in northern India to spend two weeks giving their full attention to the pursuit and discovery of enlightenment. In recent years, it was the discovery of that which I had spoken with the Rinpoche about, the impersonal nature of existence, to which I was pointing the attention of those who came to see me. It was through the discovery of that impersonal dimension of perception that the true and right relationship of all things was revealed. It was that that thrilled me so deeply, answered every question and made all things possible. Indeed, it seemed as if all of my experiences, first as a seeker and then as a teacher, had been leading me to this.

Soon I would be returning to Kathmandu and then I was off to New Zealand. What an adventure! There was now a worldwide community of hundreds of people who were willing to dedicate their lives to proving that the miracle of enlightenment made true love possible in a love-starved world.

My inability to compromise, coupled with intense curiosity and a willingness to be independent, has taken me to a place that would have been impossible to imagine even only a few short years ago. Sometimes I truly feel that I must have lost my mind, that I must be crazy. But most of the time, it seems like the riddle of human existence has been solved, that the mystery of ignorance has been demystified, and most importantly, that the way to profound and meaningful sanity has been found.

It's often too much to believe. It's too much to take in. It almost seems like it couldn't be possible.

For more information about Andrew Cohen and his teaching please contact:

Moksha Foundation
P.O. Box 5265
Larkspur, CA 94977
USA
tel: 415-927-3210
fax: 415-927-2032

FACE Centre (Friends of Andrew Cohen in Europe)
Centre Studios
Englands Lane
London NW3 4YD
UK
tel: 44-171-483-3732
fax: 44-171-916-3170